To You I Call

To You I Call

Psalms Throughout Our Lives

RABBI JADE SANK ROSS

Foreword by
Rabbi Elyse D. Frishman

Translation by
Rabbi Richard N. Levy

RJP
CCAR
Press

Reform Judaism Publishing, a division of CCAR Press
CENTRAL CONFERENCE OF AMERICAN RABBIS
5785 · NEW YORK · 2024

Published by Reform Judaism Publishing, a division of CCAR Press
Central Conference of American Rabbis
355 Lexington Avenue, New York, NY 10017
(212) 972-3636 | info@ccarpress.org | www.ccarpress.org

Translations of psalms are adapted from *Songs Ascending: The Book of Psalms* by Rabbi Richard N.
Levy (CCAR Press, 2017).

LIBRARY OF CONGRESS CATALOGING-IN-PUBLICATION DATA
Names: Sank Ross, Jade, 1990-author. | Frishman, Elyse D., writer of foreword. |
 Levy, Richard N., translator.
Title: To you I call: Psalms throughout our lives / Rabbi Jade Sank Ross;
 foreword by Rabbi Elyse D. Frishman ; translation by Rabbi Richard N. Levy.
Description: New York: Reform Judaism Publishing, a division of CCAR Press, 5785 = 2024. |
 "Translations of psalms are adapted from Songs Ascending: The Book of Psalms by Rabbi
 Richard N. Levy (CCAR Press, 2017)"—Title page verso. | Summary: "The book pairs seventy-
 two psalms with a range of life moments, from giving birth to retirement to experiencing
 antisemitism—times of grief and gratitude, anticipation and despair, pain, and relief"
 —Provided by publisher.
Identifiers: LCCN 2024013463 (print) | LCCN 2024013464 (ebook) |
 ISBN 9780881236453 (trade paperback) | ISBN 9780881236460 (ebook)
Subjects: LCSH: Bible. Psalms—Meditations. | Jewish meditations. |
 Spiritual healing. | Spiritual life—Judaism.
Classification: LCC BS1430.54 .S26 2025 (print) | LCC BS1430.54 (ebook) |
 DDC 296.7/2—dc23/eng20240809
LC record available at https://lccn.loc.gov/2024013463
LC ebook record available at https://lccn.loc.gov/2024013464

Interior book design and typography by Scott-Martin Kosofsky
 at The Philidor Company, www.philidor.com.
Cover art: *Gates of Jerusalem* (2004) © Rachel Braun, www.rachelbraun.net.
 Photo by Philip Brookman.

Printed in U.S.A.
10 9 8 7 6 5 4 3 2 1

This book is lovingly dedicated in honor of
Rabbi Jade Sank Ross
by her family, friends, colleagues,
and community members.

Ann and Fred Axelrod
The Bandler Family
Doreen and Michael Berne
Mace Blicksilver
Jane and Michael Broido
Lenore and Robert Bronstein
   and Family
The Brous Family
Miriam and Robert Caslow
The Clergy of Central Synagogue
The Coben-Freehof Family
Charlotte and David Cohen
The Clergy of
   The Community Synagogue
Sisterhood of
   The Community Synagogue
The Dell Family
Jill and Mark Eisenberg
The Epstein Family
Lyuba and Larry Feinblum
The Franchetti-Gardberg Family
The Garfin Family
Rabbi Maya Y. Glasser
Rabbi Howard Goldsmith
The Gordon Family
Tara and Josh Greenspan
Nancy and Steve Kaplan
The Katz Family
Susan Kaufman

Rabbis Samuel Kaye
   and Taylor Baruchel
The Kindler Family
The Klarman Family
Linda Kulla
Judy Levy
Rabbi Jennifer Mangold
Carol Musumeci and
   Elizabeth Olesh
The Nemitoff-Bresler Family
Susan H. Picker, PhD
The Raber Family
The Clergy of Congregation
   Rodeph Sholom
Beth and Michael Ross
Carol and David Sank
Becky and David Schamis
The Seltzer Family
Debbie Shlafmitz
Stefanie Shulman and
   Mark Calem
Mara and Baron Silverstein
Karen and Todd Sloan
Valerie and Andrew Steinberg
The Stern Family
Esther and Dan Tanenbaum
Pam and Larry Tarica
Tessie Travin
The Tuthill Family
Bari Ziegel and Gary Weiss

Contents

Foreword   xi
Rabbi Elyse D. Frishman
Acknowledgments   xv
Introduction   xvii

PSALMS FOR ANTICIPATION

Making Life-Changing Decisions: Psalm 1   3
Before Major Transitions: Psalm 118   4
While Waiting for Important News: Psalm 9   6
Taking or Receiving Results of a Major Exam: Psalm 46   8
Before Entering Stressful Situations: Psalm 59   10
Before Marching for Social Change: Psalm 50   12
Before an Election: Psalm 111   14
When Caregiving: Psalm 55   15
Before or After Surgery: Psalm 20   17
Beginning Hospice Care: Psalm 73   18
Going to the Mikveh: Psalm 77   20
Before Traveling: Psalm 138   22
A Long-Anticipated Meeting: Psalm 133   23
Praying for the Growth of an Embryo: Psalm 37   24
Beginning a Process of Expanding One's Family: Psalm 144   27

PSALMS FOR COMMEMORATION

Shivah—The Week After Losing a Beloved: Psalm 3   31
Sh'loshim—The Month After Losing a Beloved: Psalm 13   32
At the Grave of a Beloved: Psalm 91   33
Unveiling: Psalm 104   35
Yahrzeit—A Year After Losing a Beloved: Psalm 121   38
Remembering a Life-Changing Loss: Psalm 131   39
Remembering a Traumatic Event: Psalm 137   40
Choosing to End a Pregnancy: Psalm 27   41
Anniversaries: Psalm 117   43
Marking Time Since or Leading to Moving: Psalm 105   44

PSALMS FOR DESPAIR

    Accepting Death: Psalm 63   49
    The Day After Losing a Beloved: Psalm 23   50
    Experiencing a Significant Loss for the First Time: Psalm 61   51
    Mourning Multiple Losses: Psalm 62   52
    When We Fail: Psalm 130   54
    When Leaving, Separating, or Divorcing: Psalm 103   55
    After Losing a Wanted Pregnancy: Psalm 31   57
    Experiencing Infertility: Psalm 34   60

PSALMS FOR GRATITUDE

    Birthdays: Psalm 119   65
    Graduations: Psalm 113   75
    Professional Achievements: Psalm 128   76
    Retirement: Psalm 112   77
    Moving into a New Home
        or Making Changes to a Home: Psalm 122   78
    Marriage: Psalm 100   79
    Pregnancy: Psalm 139   80
    After Giving Birth: Psalm 115   82
    At a Naming Ceremony: Psalm 8   84
    When a Child Reaches a Milestone of Adulthood: Psalm 84   85
    Looking Back on a Life-Changing Moment: Psalm 5   87
    Making It Safely out of a Precarious Situation: Psalm 28   89
    Reuniting After a Long Separation: Psalm 147   90
    After Studying a Jewish Text: Psalm 78   92
    Traveling to Israel: Psalm 126   97

PSALMS FOR PAIN

    From Health to Illness: Psalm 6   101
    Loss of an Ability: Psalm 90   103
    Calling Out for Healing: Psalm 40   105
    Experiencing a Climate Disaster: Psalm 29   107
    Experiencing Antisemitism, Racism, Discrimination,
        or Hate: Psalm 39   109
    Experiencing Political Violence: Psalm 74   111
    In Times of Abuse: Psalm 18   113

In Times of Pain: Psalm 41   117

In Times of Loneliness: Psalm 88   119

In Times of War or Conflict: Psalm 140   121

After an Argument: Psalm 143   123

PSALMS FOR RELIEF

From Illness to Health: Psalm 16   127

Surviving an Accident: Psalm 92   128

For Sobriety or Changing a Habit: Psalm 33   130

After Coming Out/Inviting In: Psalm 94   132

Living into Our Identities: Psalm 4   134

Holding a Child for the First Time: Psalm 45   135

Feeding a Child: Psalm 136   137

Experiencing Success After Hard Work: Psalm 67   139

Accepting a New Job: Psalm 72   140

Paying Off a Debt: Psalm 66   142

After Planning a Major Event: Psalm 48   144

Moments of Respite: Psalm 19   146

Before Going on Vacation: Psalm 24   148

Index of Psalms   149

About the Author   151

Foreword

RABBI ELYSE D. FRISHMAN

LIFE IS JOYFUL, tragic, visionary, mired in muck. Hope is our light in the darkest night.

There's eschatological hope: things will get better, and maybe we will understand the reason behind the madness. Then there's Jewish hope: *tikvah*, deep connection. *Tikvah* is God's promise that we are never alone.

But sometimes we wonder: Is there God?

One doesn't sense the absence of God through reason; it begins with emotion. Something breaks our assumptions about goodness, meaning, and purpose.

When we learned that our daughter had been killed, we collapsed. Time and space meant nothing. Yet, there was light. Friends and strangers surrounded us gently. God was patient with our terror. Love held us.

I thought of the driver who hit our daughter. Who among us hasn't focused on that yellow light and pushed the accelerator a little bit harder? He didn't see her—and she didn't see him. What he would live with for the rest of his life . . . Though I couldn't comprehend the depth of my own pain, I could forgive. I called him before the funeral.

How would I get through the funeral, burial, shivah? I was terrified, yet I wasn't existentially afraid. Psalm 23:4 called me: "Even when I walk in a valley dark as death's shadow, I shall fear no evil." Our daughter's *n'shamah* (spirit) was embraced. I looked for signs—and there were signs. I looked for her—and wept and wept and wept. "You are with me, Your staff and Your walking stick—they reassure me." The psalm took my grief and held my hand.

There has never been a time when we humans haven't suffered. Sometimes it's the random act of nature. More often, human action breaks our hearts. We have little control over life. We manage the best that we can. We fight, we nurture, and we love messily. Maybe we become wise.

We choose life despite its persistent infidelity. The psalms sing of this choice in all circumstances. They remind us that God created us in love.

So: Why isn't it all good? Why do we suffer?

Psalm 103:10–11 sings:

> God has not dealt with us according to our sins,
> Nor bestowed on us the consequences of our iniquities.
> For as high as the heavens are above the earth,
> So powerful is God's covenantal love
> Over those who revere God's name.

God loves us in all our complexity. "Hold on. I'm here. You're not alone. You matter, even now. Even as nothing is understandable or meaningful. Selah. Breathe." Yes, we are the center of the universe.

And, no, we are *not* the center of the *spiritual* universe. We are a constellation of spirits seeking oneness within the ether of the Higher.

Psalm 118:5–9:

> From within the narrow space I cried out: "Yah! [God!]"
> The Holy One answered me in Yah's expansive space.
> I have Adonai, no need to dread—
> What can others have of me?
> I have Adonai for help,
> So I can stare down my assailants!
> It is good to take refuge in Adonai—
> Better than trusting in peers;
> It is good to take refuge in Adonai—
> Better than trusting in princes.

We know the danger of trusting in human leadership, and we recognize our own personal unreliability. Better to look beyond the corporeal, to the light that ignites the spirit. We close our eyes to see. Rest in the embrace of the Higher. Selah. Breathe.

The Hebrew—and original—term for psalms is *t'hillim*, meaning "praises." A *t'hillah* sings to the Higher, promising that we are heard. Selah.

Psalms are songs of life, callings and connections to the Higher.

Why "psalm"? It's from the Greek *psallein*, "pluck," and *psalmos*, a song accompanied by the harp. Several psalms begin, "To the conductor," as an instruction to the one who would lead music in the glorious Jerusalem Temple. In our day, we might sing to the Conductor on High: the One who plucks our heartstrings and orchestrates the pain and joy in our lives. The score is written by us; the Conductor holds us together. And like a junior high school band concert, the sound can be cacophonous when our skills are in formation. The more we practice, the better our skill, the better our orchestral performance in life. With our finest form, the Conductor will shape glorious music.

May we recite psalms if we don't believe?

My teacher Rabba Saphir Noyman Eyal explains, "If you perceive the distance, you can come closer." True faith isn't naive. It emerges from struggle. Jacob wrestled. Aaron was silent in grief *and* remained the High Priest. Job tossed and turned in the nightmare of tragic loss, with friends who were like foes. Each understood that their tests weren't about *having* faith but the *quality* of faith: What were their expectations? And what were the expectations of the Higher for each of them?

It's difficult to think like this, to believe like this. Our era heightens the importance of the self. Yet self-awareness must grow into us-awareness, with love for the other. Love for the other is the true context for meaningful life. Love for the other ensures hope. This is what the psalms offer us.

Why does a patient feel hope when a circle of friends offers psalms? Why before an interview or difficult conversation might one open these songs? Why in grief? In celebration? Anticipation?

During shivah, the seven days of intense mourning following burial, a colleague sent me her favorite translation of psalms, highlighting those she thought would be most helpful. That gift is what Rabbi Sank Ross has done for us in this volume. She has shone light on key psalms to support us in a myriad of times, from the tragic to the celebratory.

She chose 72 psalms out of 150. The poet Zelda wrote (as translated by Dr. Marcia Falk), "Each of us has a name." We are named by our woes and our wins, our losses and loves. We have titles and tender endearments: Rabbi, Dr., Honey, Sweetheart. Did you know that God has seventy-two names? Like a multifaceted jewel, there are seventy-two aspects that shine, each a bit differently. There are seventy-two connections with the Higher, mood-dependent on us.

Rabbi Sank Ross selected these seventy-two psalms for us to experience the hand of God. Like walking out into a too-bright day, then putting on sunglasses, and suddenly seeing more clearly, so Rabbi Sank Ross invites us to try on something new to experience life more intentionally.

Rabbi Sank Ross was my student at the Barnert Temple, growing from youth to awareness. Her brilliant eyes scanned everywhere to absorb, learn, and understand. She questioned, she struggled, and she formed a deep love for our people and faith.

Jade, you sing from the depths of knowing. With your offering *To You I Call*, you invite us to find our places in God's compassionate embrace.

For you, Psalm 128:

> A Song of Ascendings.
> Happy is everyone who holds God in awe,
> Who walks in God's ways.
> When you eat from the toil of your hands,
> Happy will you be and it will be good for you . . .
> Your boys and girls will be like olive shoots
> All around your table.
> Behold—thus shall the person be blessed
> Who holds God in awe.
> May Adonai bless you from Zion
> And may you look upon the good of Jerusalem
> All the days of your life,
> Beholding children for your children—
> Peace upon Israel!

The teacher loves to become the student. Thank you for your precious gift.

Rabbi Elyse D. Frishman is Rabbi Emerita at the Barnert Temple in Franklin Lakes, New Jersey. She is the editor of *Mishkan T'filah: A Reform Siddur*, published by CCAR Press.

Acknowledgments

MANY THANKS TO RABBI RICHARD N. LEVY for taking us all to new heights with his translations of all 150 psalms in *Songs Ascending*.

To the Editorial Advisory Committee: I hope you realize the depth of the impact that each of you had on this book. Thank you for bringing your full selves and whole hearts to this project. I am in your debt for your many gifts of time, patience, insight, and wisdom.

Thank you to my *chavruta* Rabbi Josh Warshawsky. Your friendship, creativity, and gift for composition illuminates the depths and nuances of our sacred texts, shaping my understanding of their wisdom and enriching my own writing.

Thank you to Rabbi Elyse D. Frishman for writing this book's foreword. As a writer and editor of liturgy and a leader in the Reform Movement and beyond, your rabbinate has, in so many ways, inspired my own. From the time I was a child in Barnert Temple's religious school until you placed Rabbi Bernard Zlotowitz (*z"l*) and Rabbi Martin Rozenberg's (*z"l*) *The Book of Psalms: The New Translation and Commentary of the Psalms* in my hands in 2017 at the very start of my exploration of the psalms, you have been with me every step of the way. I cannot imagine anyone else writing the foreword of this book. I am filled with gratitude that you are part of my life and chose to be part of this project.

To the staff of the CCAR Press, the impact you have on all of us is immeasurable. With each and every word, you sustain worlds. Thank you for humbly guiding and inspiring me.

Rabbi Hara Person, Chief Executive of the CCAR
Rafael Chaiken, Director of the Press
Rabbi Anne Villarreal-Belford, Editor
Chiara Ricisak, Assistant Editor
Deborah Smilow, Press Operations Manager
Raquel Fairweather-Gallie, Marketing and Sales Manager

Thank you also to copyeditor Debra Hirsch Corman, designer Scott-Martin Kosofsky, proofreader Michelle Kwitkin, and cover designer Barbara Leff.

As a rabbinical student at Hebrew Union College–Jewish Institute of Religion, Rabbi Sonja K. Pilz, PhD, guided me with her incredible breadth of knowledge, wisdom, and creativity in reimagining what a rabbinic thesis could be. In 2018, with Sonja as my advisor, I completed my inter-departmental rabbinic capstone project, "The Psalms as Living Liturgy." A year later, Sonja suggested that I consider expanding this project into a book. I owe an immense debt of gratitude to Sonja for all that she gave to this project, from its very beginning on the third floor of 1 West Fourth Street, to the writing of the proposal, to the book's completion. Thank you for being my teacher, for seeing me, and for encouraging me to share my *torah*.

To my parents, Carol and David Sank, thank you for the countless sacrifices you make, the endless time you give, and the unconditional support you lend so that I can pursue my calling as a rabbi. It is because of you that I am the person I am today. I am endlessly grateful.

To Adina and Bella who came into my life as this book came into being, you are a reminder of the wonder that surrounds us. "For now I see Your heavens, the work of Your fingers, moon and stars which you prepared" (Psalm 8:4). Thank you for the light that you bring to me and to this world just by being you.

My dearest, Rabbi Dan Ross—without your support, encouragement, endless willingness to listen to and discuss my ideas, and your partnership as my co-parent, this project never would have been possible. Thank you for choosing me to be your *chavruta* in life, for all the adventures we have already begun together, and for all those yet to come.

Introduction

THE GENESIS for this book followed the completion of my rabbinic capstone project. This project—the culmination of my five years of rabbinic study—was, as far as I know, the first of its kind at Hebrew Union College–Jewish Institute of Religion in New York, combining a comprehensive, immersive study of the Book of Psalms with a presentation of an original *Hallel*—"set of psalms"—selected to be incorporated into a *Shacharit* (morning) service. The psalms I selected addressed the current moment through text, music, and digital images in the context of prayer.

While working on this project, engaging in the ancient practice of reading daily psalms, I started to see the psalms everywhere: in synagogues, at archaeological sites in Israel, in artwork, and in music. Their texts accompanied me every day. Their words became meaningful in situations when I found myself speechless and searching for words. I found that the psalms respond to human nature in a unique way. The language of the psalms is open enough to allow space for all of us to "come as we are" and to take what we need. The psalms also belong to American society as a whole: they are part of both the Hebrew and the Christian Bible, they appear widely in both our religious and secular culture, and their universal themes of fear, suffering, and rejoicing reach all people. The psalms enable us to access our spirituality at any given moment and in ways that speak to our souls.

As I incorporated psalms into places where I felt the set liturgy did not address contemporary experiences, I realized that a resource connecting the psalms to experiences in our lives, whether on an average day or one with unique pain or joy, would be very useful for the creation of rituals and worship. Additionally, such a book would be a rich spiritual resource for the personal practice of anyone seeking modern connections to our ancient sources. The volume in your hands aims to do exactly that: it pairs our traditional psalms with different moments of our contemporary lives.

My vision is that this volume will make the psalms more accessible and easier to navigate so they can be seamlessly incorporated into formal worship and other moments of personal prayer. This, in turn, will create opportunities to deepen Jewish spirituality, since these psalms accompany anyone on any occasion: at home, in the hospital, by the graveside, while traveling, or during meditation. Finally, this volume and the psalms within it will, I hope, empower you to establish a meaningful, personal prayer practice, whether regularly or occasionally.

To meet the vision I have for this book, it was important to make this book easy to navigate by narrowing down the 150 psalms to 72 (four times eighteen, quadruple *chai*/life) and dividing the 72 psalms featured here thematically into six broad categories—anticipation, commemoration, despair, gratitude, pain, and relief. Each category is then further divided into specific moments and experiences, such as "Looking Back on a Life-Changing Moment," "Experiencing a Climate Disaster," or "While Waiting for Important News."

The psalms can be divided in many ways. The Psalter may be divided numerically into five books, each ending with a doxology or words of praise to God, as Nahum Sarna explains in his book *On the Book of Psalms*.[1] They can be divided into groupings by title, author, or heading. In their first lines, many of the psalms are attributed to an author such as David or Asaph, while others begin with musical instructions like "For the conductor: On strings." There are other ways to divide the psalms based on the ways that they have been and are used. For example, the *maalot* psalms, 120–134, all begin with the words *Shir HaMaalot*, "A Song of Ascendings," and it is believed that these are the psalms that may have been sung by pilgrims as they journeyed to Jerusalem or even ascended the steps of the Temple. Today, we continue to recite what we call *Hallel*, Psalms 113–118, in synagogues on festive occasions. These are the same psalms our ancestors may have recited as they made their sacrifices during the festivals of Pesach, Shavuot, and Sukkot. Additionally, scholars of the psalms have divided them into many other categories by theme or content. In *The Book of Psalms*, Robert Alter divides the psalms into several categories including praise, supplication, thanksgiving, wisdom, and Zion.[2] Walter Brueggemann, in his *The Message of the Psalms*, divides the psalms into three categories: psalms of orientation, psalms of disorientation, and psalms of new orientation; he explains that we are all constantly in a state of movement from orientation to disorientation and from disorientation to new orientation.[3] In this way, Brueggemann explains that the psalms are "both sides of the conversation of faith"[4]—our side and God's.

As I categorized the psalms, some clearly called to be linked with certain occasions, and then there were additional occasions that in turn called out for psalms. Clearly, by making these decisions, I made assumptions about your emotional responses to particular moments. You might find these inaccurate or one-dimensional. To help guide you toward a psalm that might ring more true for you, I offer suggestions in the footnotes of each psalm to at least one other psalm included in this book. I invite you to look for what you are feeling at any moment—beyond the way I have divided the contents, beyond the specifics of the occasions identified here, including among the remaining seventy-eight psalms that are not in this book.

As the psalms are ancient sources, there are some inherent challenges in reading them today and applying them to our present moment. Throughout this volume, you might notice transliterated Hebrew words that are not translated into English, such as *michtam* in Psalm 16 and *Mut-laben* in Psalm 9. Most of these transliterated words refer to technical musical instructions whose exact meanings have been lost, so they are presented in the original Hebrew through transliteration. Similarly, you will see that the Hebrew words for God appear in transliteration as well, such as the words "Adonai" and "Yah." Much like the English word "God," these Hebrew words offer an invitation to imagine the Divine in any way that we find meaningful. Additionally, the psalms sometimes contain problematic texts and metaphors that may not speak to us in the twenty-first century. These include, but are not limited to, descriptions of violence, vengeance against enemies, gendered language, and theologies that do not resonate with our own (for example, Psalm 137:9, "Joyful the one who seizes your children and shatters them against the rock"). When reading the psalms, I often find myself focusing on just one or a few verses; this alleviates the tension and allows me to take what I need from the psalms and release problematic texts. To help guide you through this challenge, I chose one verse from each psalm included in this book, which you will see featured in Hebrew at the top of the page as well as in bold lettering in the English translation. I also wrote *kavanot*, prayerful intentions, to help connect moments from our lives with these ancient words. You are welcome to start with the *kavanah*, focus on the verse in bold lettering , or read the full psalm and find others that you connect with.

Remember, too, that psalms are poetry, and almost all poetry is metaphor. The beauty of metaphors is that they can be redefined. Perhaps you could consider problematic texts as invitations to reinterpret and redefine the metaphors and even to write your own psalms. Some books that might help you in this approach include *New Each Day: A Spiritual Practice for Reading Psalms* by Rabbi Debra Robbins, *Flames to Heaven: New Psalms for Healing and Praise* by Debbie Perlman, and *Talking to God: Personal Prayers for Times of Joy, Sadness, Struggle, and Celebration* by Rabbi Naomi Levy.[5]

The translations in this book are adapted from *Songs Ascending* by Rabbi Richard N. Levy, published by the CCAR Press.[6] Rabbi Levy's English translations are poetic yet clear and largely preserve the intentions of the original Hebrew. For me, where *Songs Ascending* really meets the work of *To You I Call* is not in the unique translations themselves, but rather in Rabbi Levy's richly spiritual commentary, where he raises questions like "How might this psalm articulate an aspect of our spiritual lives . . . help us celebrate a a holiday or another special day? How might it accompany us when we are ill, or visiting someone who is ill? How might it provide comfort when we have lost someone dear to us?"[7] I turned to the psalms because I was looking to answer exactly these questions. What I needed was a concise resource to inspire me. My hope is that the volume in your hands will be exactly this: a resource and a space to see the psalms as poetry, prayer, and song to inspire our spiritual journeys. I encourage you to turn to *Songs Ascending* and its meaningful notes when you have a question about Rabbi Levy's translations, as that commentary and explanation is beyond the scope of this book.

The title of this book, *To You I Call*, is taken from Rabbi Levy's translation of Psalm 30. It captures the spirit of the psalms and applies to many of the situations and moments included within these pages. I hope it calls to you.

NOTES

1. Nahum M. Sarna, *On the Book of Psalms: Exploring the Prayers of Ancient Israel* (New York: Schocken Books, 1993), 15–16.
2. Robert Alter, *The Book of Psalms: A Translation with Commentary* (New York: W.W. Norton, 2007), xvii–xviii.
3. Walter Brueggemann, *The Message of the Psalms: A Theological Commentary* (Minneapolis: Augsburg, 1984).
4. Brueggeman, *Message of the Psalms*, 15, 19–23.
5. Debra J. Robbins, *New Each Day: A Spiritual Practice for Reading Psalms* (CCAR Press, 2024); Debbie Perlman, *Flames to Heaven: New Psalms for Healing and Praise* (Rad Publishers, 1998); Naomi Levy, *Talking to God: Personal Prayers for Times of Joy, Sadness, Struggle, and Celebration* (Doubleday, 2002).
6. Richard N. Levy, *Songs Ascending: The Book of Psalms in a New Translation with Textual and Spiritual Commentary* (New York: CCAR Press, 2017), xvii.
7. Levy, *Songs Ascending*, xvii.

Psalms for Anticipation

At times, we stand in the doorway to what is next, at a moment of significant change. We hold seemingly opposite emotions at once: fear and confidence; anxiety and serenity; despair and hope. We look for words of comfort and affirmation to stay with us and guide us forward.

וְהָיָה כְּעֵץ שָׁתוּל עַל־פַּלְגֵי־מָיִם

Making Life-Changing Decisions

PSALM 1

In this moment of discernment we look for wisdom to guide us. This psalm asks that as we seek the Divine as a guiding source, we may be able to align ourselves with righteousness to make decisions that lead us to inner peace.

1 *Ashrei ha-ish*:
   Happy is the one who has not walked
   In the counsel of the wicked
   And in the path of sinners has not stood,
   And in a chamber of cheats has not sat down,
2 Finding delight instead
   In the Torah of Adonai,
   Reflecting on that Torah in daytime and the dark.
3 **Like such a person is a tree planted by a stream of water,**
   Offering its fruit when the time is ripe,
   Leafy at all times, never withering.
   Whatever it produces
   Lasts.
4 Not like this are the wicked,
   They are like chaff instead,
   Scattered by the wind.
5 Therefore the wicked cannot withstand judgment
   Nor can sinners stand in a community of the just,
6 For Adonai knows the path of the just
   But the path of the wicked will disappear.

▶ See also Psalm 28.

עָזִּי וְזִמְרָת יָהּ וַיְהִי־לִי לִישׁוּעָה:

Before Major Transitions
PSALM 118

As we prepare for any life-changing transition or change, we pray to approach transformations ahead with courage and hope. May these words steady us as we continue to discover our unfolding paths, so we may fully embrace with authenticity and joy the beauty of who we are.

1 Give thanks to Adonai, who is good,
   For eternal is God's covenantal love!

2 O let Israel say:
   Eternal is God's covenantal love!

3 O let the House of Aaron say:
   For eternal is God's covenantal love!

4 O let those who revere Adonai say:
   For eternal is God's covenantal love!

5 From within the narrow space I cried out: Yah!
   The Holy One answered me in Yah's expansive space.

6 I have Adonai, no need to dread—
   What can others have of me?

7 I have Adonai for help,
   So I can stare down my assailants!

8 It is good to take refuge in Adonai—
   Better than trusting in peers;

9 It is good to take refuge in Adonai—
   Better than trusting in princes.

10 All the peoples have surrounded me?
   With the name of Adonai I will cut them off!

11 They have surrounded me—they have made
   circles around me?
   With the name of Adonai I will cut them off!

12 They have surrounded me like bees?
 They will dry up like thorns in a fire!
 With the name of Adonai I will cut them off!
13 You made me stumble and fall,
 But God helped me.
14 **My strength and song is Yah,**
 Who is my deliverance!
15 The sound of melody and deliverance is in the tents of the just:
 The right hand of Adonai acts bravely!
16 The right hand of Adonai is raised high,
 The right hand of Adonai acts bravely!
17 I shall not die—no, I shall live,
 And tell tales of the works of Yah:
18 Yah afflicted me—agonizingly afflicted me—
 But did not give me over to death!
19 So open the gates of righteousness for me—
 I'm coming through them to give thanks to Yah!
20 This is the gate for Adonai,
 The just are coming through it!

▶ See also Psalms 4 and 77.

לֹא־שָׁכַ֖ח צַעֲקַ֣ת עֲנָוִֽים׃

While Waiting for Important News

PSALM 9

This psalm speaks of God as our refuge and stronghold in times of trouble. As we hold space in our waiting, we pray for strength, fortitude, and faith—whatever the outcome of this moment.

1 To the conductor: On *Mut-laben*,
   A psalm of David.

2 Adonai I praise with all my heart;
   All Your wonders will I in tales recount.

3 Applause and shouts of joy I offer You,
   Anthems to Your name I sing: Most High!

4 Backwards turn my enemies,
   They fall over themselves,
   They perish from Your presence.

5 For You have rendered a judgment of justice for me,
   You have sat on the bench as a just judge,

6 Censuring the nations, destroying the wicked;
   You have blotted out their name from time and space.

7 Enemies are ended, turned to eternal desolation,
   Their cities You uprooted, every trace of them is destroyed.

8 Forever Adonai shall dwell,
   On a throne You have prepared for judgment.

9 For You judge the planet with justice,
   You try the nations with uprightness.

10 For Adonai will be a fortress for the oppressed,
    A fortress in times in trouble.

11 For those familiar with Your name will trust in You
    Since You have not abandoned those who seek You, Adonai.

12 Glad songs sing out to Adonai, who dwells in Zion;
    Tell tales of God's deeds among the nations!

13 For the One who attends to bloodshedders keeps these in mind:
God has not forgotten the groaning of humble people.

14 Have favor upon me, Adonai;
See what I suffer from those who hate me,
You who pull me from the portals of the sleep of death

15 That I might tell Your praise-stories
At the portals of Daughter Zion—
How I will rejoice in the victory You have brought me!

16 In the pit they have made, the nations sink down;
In this net where they hid, their own foot is caught.

17 Adonai is known, having done justice—
Transgressors are trapped through the work of their hands.
Selah!

18 Jaws of Sheol greet the backsliding transgressor
Along with all peoples who forget there is God.

19 *Keep your faith*: the needy will not be forgotten forever!
The hope of the poor will not perish, not ever.

20 Arise, Adonai—let not mere mortals prevail,
Let nations be judged by Your presence.

21 Bestow, Adonai, terror for them—
Let peoples know:
Mere mortals are they, selah!

▶ See also Psalms 33 and 130.

Taking or Receiving Results of a Major Exam

PSALM 46

Whether anticipating taking a major exam or receiving the results, anxiety is high in this moment. Psalm 46 speaks of God as a refuge as we search for inner stillness and peace in the face of the unknown. No matter the result, we pray that we will find resilience and be open to many possibilities and paths ahead.

1 For the conductor: for the sons of Korach,
   Al Alamot. A song.
2 God is for us a refuge and strength,
   A help found easily when troubles come.
3 **Therefore we shall not fear when the earth reels,**
   Or when the mountains totter into the heart of the seas,
4 When its waters roar and rage,
   When the mountains shake as the seas rise up—selah!
5 A river: its channels bring joy to the city of God,
   The most holy of the dwelling places of the Most High.
6 God is in her midst, she shall not totter;
   God will help her as darkness turns toward morning.
7 Peoples roared—kingdoms tottered;
   God gave forth a sound—the earth began to melt!
8 Adonai of hosts is with us,
   A high tower for us is the God of Jacob—selah!
9 Go, behold the works of Adonai
   Who has brought barren places to the earth,
10 Abolished wars to the end of the earth,
   Broken the bow and severed the spear,
   Burned up chariots in a blazing conflagration.

11 "Let them go, and know that I am God—
   I am high above the nations, I am high above the earth!"
12 "Adonai of hosts is with us,
   A high tower for us is the God of Jacob—selah!"

▶ See also Psalms 119 and 121.

עָזֹּו אֵלֶיךָ אֶשְׁמֹרָה כִּי־אֱלֹהִים מִשְׂגַּבִּי:

Before Entering Stressful Situations

PSALM 59

In times of stress, this psalm steadies us with assurance of God's unwavering presence and protection. May this bring us strength and fortitude.

1 For the conductor: "Do Not Destroy," of David.
   A *michtam*, when at Saul's instigation they were watching David's
      house to kill him.

2 Deliver me from my enemies, O God of mine—
   Fortify me against those who rise up against me!

3 Deliver me from the workers of wrongdoing—
   Bring me victory against men of blood!

4 For behold, they lie in wait for me,
   The strongmen hang around me.
   This is not my rebelliousness nor my sin, Adonai.

5 With no wrong on my part, they run and get themselves ready—
   Be stirred on my behalf, and look!

6 After all, You are Adonai, God of hosts, the God of Israel—
   Arouse Yourself to punish all the nations!
   Shed no grace on iniquitous traitors—selah!

7 They come back in the evening, they growl like contempt,
   They roam around the city;

8 Drool hangs from their mouths, swords from their lips—
   "Who is listening?"

9 Thou shalt laugh at them, Adonai—
   You poke fun at all the peoples.

10 **God is the Strong One—I shall watch for You,**
   For God is my fortress.

11 The loving God of my covenant will go before me;
   God will let me look out at those who are watching me.

12 Do not kill them, lest my people forget—
   Let them become wanderers through Your might,
      and bring them down,
   Adonai my shield!

13 For the sin of their mouth, the word of their lips,
   Let them be captured in their arrogance
   Amidst their vile oaths and the lies they tell.
14 Consume them in wrath, consume them, let them be no more—
   That they may know that God rules in Jacob
   To the ends of the earth—selah!
15 Still they come back in the evening, they growl with contempt,
   They roam around the city;
16 They wander in search of food;
   If they are not satisfied, they will stay all night.
17 But I shall sing of Your strength,
   My voice shall burst forth in the morning in praise of Your
      covenantal love,
   For You have been my fortress
   And my refuge in the day I am distressed.
18 O my strength, to You I offer melodies,
   For God is my fortress, the loving God of my covenant.

▶ See also Psalms 6 and 9.

יָגִּידוּ שָׁמַיִם צִדְקוֹ כִּי־אֱלֹהִים שֹׁפֵט הוּא סֶלָה׃

Before Marching for Social Change

PSALM 50

This psalm fills us with conviction and courage, reminding us of God's call to do justice, love mercy, and walk humbly. As we fight for change today, may we remember the sacrifices that have been made to reach this moment and the importance of personal transformation and self-reflection in the fight for justice. We pray that we will truly make a difference in the world.

1 A psalm of Asaph.
God
God
Gracious Adonai
Has spoken and called, "Earth!"
From the going forth of the sun to its coming in.
2 From Zion, perfection of beauty,
Has God burst forth.
3 God is entering, and does not keep silent.
A fire consumes everything before the Holy One—
It rages wildly all around!
4 God calls to the heavens from above,
And to the earth, to judge the people:
5 "Gather to Me all those bound by My covenant—
All those who, through offerings, have cut a covenant with Me!"
6 **Let the heavens tell tales of God's justice,**
For God *is* the judge—selah!
7 "Listen to Me that I may speak,
O Israel—and I shall testify against you.
God—your God—am I.
8 Not on account of your offerings shall I reprove you,
Nor for your burnt offerings that are daily before Me.
9 I shall not take a bullock out of your house
Or he-goats from your pens.
10 For every forest-creature is Mine already—
All the cattle on a thousand hills.

11 I know intimately every bird of the mountains,
    All that moves through the fields are with Me.
12 If I were hungry, I would not speak to you.
    For the earth and its fullness are Mine.
13 Do I consume the flesh of animals?
    The blood of he-goats—do I drink it?
14 Offer to God an offering of gratitude,
    And make good your vows to the Most High!
15 Call upon Me in a day of trouble;
    I will deliver you, and then you can honor Me."
16 But to the wicked God has said:
    "What is it to you to tell about My statutes
    And to take My covenant into Your mouth?
17 For you hate reproof,
    And you have cast My words away from you.
18 If you saw a thief, you ran with him,
    And found your portion with those committing adultery.
19 You have sent your mouth to do evil
    And you have yoked your tongue to deceit.
20 You sit there and speak against your brother—
    Against your own mother's son you attribute fault.
21 These things you have done—and should I keep silent?
    You thought of *Ehyeh* being like you!
    I shall rebuke you and set out the case before your eyes.
22 Please, understand this, you who are forgetting God,
    Lest I tear in pieces and there is no one to rescue.
23 The one who offers an offering of gratitude honors Me,
    And to the one who lays a path I will show the deliverance of God."

▶ See also Psalms 33 and 111.

כֹּחַ מַעֲשָׂיו הִגִּיד לְעַמּוֹ לָתֵת לָהֶם נַחֲלַת גּוֹיִם:

Before an Election

PSALM 111

As we participate in the democratic process of electing our leaders, Psalm 111 inspires us to cast our votes with discernment, integrity, and reverence for the responsibility that comes with shaping our collective future. We pray that our elected leaders will help to build a just and compassionate society.

1 *Hall'lu-Yah!*
  All my heart will praise God
  Before the council of the upright and the congregation.
2 Copious are the works of Adonai,
  Delighting all who search them out.
3 Exalted is Your work,
  For Your justice stands forever!
4 Glory You have assured for all Your wonders—
  Hovering with grace and compassion are You, Adonai,
5 Insulating from hunger those who revere You,
  Joining together members of Your covenant forever,
6 **Keeping the power of Your deeds for Your people,**
  Lavishing the heritage of the nations upon them,
7 Making truth and justice with Your own hand,
  Numbering all Your faithful precepts,
8 Offering them as a firm foundation, now and forever,
  Produced from truth and uprightness,
9 Quenching Your people's longing for release,
  Requiring adherence to Your covenant forever—
  Sacred, awesome, is Your name.
10 The beginning of wisdom is awe for Adonai,
  Understanding and goodness belong to the doers
    of God's word;
  Zest in Your praise stands forever.

▶ See also Psalms 29 and 46.

When Caregiving

PSALM 55

The journey of caregiving can be lonely and isolating. Watching the ones we love when they are in pain or changed because of illness, we too experience loss, heartache, and sorrow. May we find the endurance and strength to continue caring for our loved ones—and ourselves—with compassion and grace.

1 For the conductor: with string-music. A *maskil* of David.

2 May my entreaty enter Your ears, God—
Do not conceal Yourself from my request for grace.

3 Give me Your attention, respond to me.
I murmur restlessly, I moan

4 From the voice of the enemy, from the pressing face of the wicked,
For they make me stumble; their wickedness is upon me,
And in anger they assault me.

5 My heart pounds inside me
And the dread of death descends upon me—

6 Awe and trembling have entered into me,
Horror is smothering me!

7 **And I said: "Would that I could take wing like the dove!**
I would soar off and find a dwelling-place,

8 Wandering—look!—far and wide.
I would spend my nights in the wilderness—selah!

9 I would hurry to my shelter
From the screaming storming squall."

10 Swallow up, Superior One, split up their speech,
For I have seen violence and strife in the city.

11 Day and night they encircle her, they're all over her walls
Wreaking ravishing wrong on her inmost parts!

12 Destruction rages in her inmost parts—
Oppression and treachery will not withdraw from her streets!

13 For it was not an enemy who shamed me—
That, I could have borne.

It was not someone who bears hatred against me, aggrandizing
    himself—
That, I could have hidden from.

14 It was *you*—a person with like value to me,
    My friend, my intimate—

15 When we were together we would share sweet secrets,
    In the house of God we would meander with the throng!

16 May destruction fall upon them,
    May they collapse into Sheol alive!
    For wicked things fill their dwellings—they fill their very core!

17 Yet I will cry to the Creator,
    And Adonai will deliver me.

18 Evening and morning and midday,
    I meditate, I moan—
    God heard my voice.

19 God ransomed me in peace from those who drew near to me
    for war,
    For there were many who had ganged up on me—

20 (God will hear, and humble them—
    The One who sits enthroned from of old—selah!)—
    People who never change, who have no fear of God.

21 My treacherous friend set her hands against people at peace
    with her,
    She trashed her covenant!

22 While she spread smooth words with her mouth, her heart drew
    near for war;
    Her words, softer than oil, are unsheathed swords.

23 Cast upon Adonai whatever you have been dealt, and God will
    sustain you,
    Never permitting the just to stumble.

24 And You, O God, take them down to the pits of the pit!
    People of blood and deceit will not live half their days,
    But I—I trust in You.

▶ See also Psalms 59 and 94.

Before or After Surgery

PSALM 20

Surgery is a time of risk and vulnerability. We put our lives in another's hands. With gratitude, but also discomfort and frustration, we awaken, foggy, in a body that does not quite feel like our own and may never be the same as it was before. This psalm acknowledges fear and even anger, yet is an overall expression of gratitude.

1 To the conductor:
A psalm of David.

2 **May Adonai respond to you on a troubled day;**
May the name "God of Jacob" lift you up,

3 Sending help to you from the holy place,
Support for you out of Zion,

4 Taking note of every meal you have offered up,
Accepting the fullness of the offerings you have burnt, selah!

5 Giving to you according to the yearnings of your heart,
Fulfilling each detail of the guidance you have given.

6 Let us sing out at your deliverance,
Stretch forth a banner in the name of our God—
"May Adonai Fulfill All Your Petitions!"

7 Now I know that Adonai has brought victory to the anointed ruler,
Responding from God's holy heaven
Through the victorious power of God's right hand.

8 These invoke chariots and these horses,
But we invoke the name of Adonai, our God.

9 These bent over and fell,
But we rose up and stood restored.

10 Adonai, bring us victory,
O Majesty! May You respond to us on the day that we call.

▶ See also Psalms 16, 28, and 92.

כָּלָה שְׁאֵרִי וּלְבָבִי צוּר־לְבָבִי וְחֶלְקִי אֱלֹהִים לְעוֹלָם:

Beginning Hospice Care

PSALM 73

Deciding to begin hospice care, whether for ourselves or on behalf of a loved one, is an emotionally fraught moment. During this time of transition, we look for assuredness that along the journey leading to this decision, we have made the best possible decisions given the circumstances. We pray for strength in the coming days and for comfort and peace for all of us.

1 A Psalm of Asaph.
  Yes, God is good for Israel,
  For the wholesome of heart;
2 As for me, my feet had almost strayed,
  I almost slipped at every step—
3 For I am jealous of the boastful ones.
  I see the peacefulness of wicked people—
4 For there are no pangs at their passing,
  Their body is healthy.
5 They do not share the toil of ordinary people,
  They are not wounded like ordinary human beings.
6 Therefore pride is a chain around their neck,
  Violence is a cloak for their frame.
7 Their eyes bulge from corpulence,
  The fantasies of their heart transgress.
8 They taunt, oppressing by their hurtful words,
  Their words come as if from On High.
9 They have hurled their mouth to the heavens,
  And their tongue patrols the earth.
10 Therefore the people return there
  And waters once full are emptied out by them.
11 They say: "How can God know?
  Is there knowledge in the Most High?"
12 Behold, these are the wicked—
  Those who are at ease in the world have attained power!

13 So I have purified my heart in vain,
   Scrubbed my hands clean in vain—
14 For I have been plagued all day,
   Chastised every morning:
15 If I said, "I will tell my tale this way,"
   Look, I would have been faithless to Your flocks.
16 When I pondered on how I might ever know this,
   It became a burden in my eyes,
17 Until I'd go into the holy gates of God,
   When I understood their ultimate undoing.
18 Surely You have set them in slippery places,
   You have hurled them into the ruins.
19 How they have become a desolation in a moment!
   Finished, diminished, consumed by terrors,
20 Like a dream when one awakes.
   Creator, when You arise You will despise their image.
21 For my heart was embittered,
   I was stabbed in my inmost parts.
22 But I was dimwitted, I did not know—
   I was an animal in Your presence.
23 Still, I am always with You,
   You have grasped my right hand.
24 You guide me with Your counsel,
   And afterward You take me with glory.
25 Who but You is there for me in heaven?
   And being with You, I have no other desires on earth.
26 **Though my flesh and my heart be spent,**
   The rock of my heart and my portion is God—forever.
27 For behold, those who are far from You shall perish;
   You destroy all who wander away from You.
28 As for me, the nearness of God is good for me,
   I have made the Superior, God, my refuge,
   That I may tell my tale of all Your creative works.

▶ See also Psalms 23 and 34.

אַתָּה הָאֵל עֹשֵׂה פֶּלֶא הוֹדַעְתָּ בָעַמִּים עֻזֶּךָ:

Going to the Mikveh

PSALM 77

As we prepare to mark time or a transition in our lives through immersion in living water, this psalm connects us with the courage and resilience of our ancestors who were transformed through water. May we feel renewed and strengthened to embrace this ritual—and the change it marks— wholeheartedly.

1 For the conductor: on *Y'dutun*, of Asaph, a psalm.

2 My voice is to God as I cry out,
My voice is to God that the Holy One may give ear to me.

3 In the day of my distress I have sought out Adonai,
My hand, stretched out at night, does not grow numb—
I refuse to be comforted.

4 I mention it, my God, and I moan;
I speak of it and my spirit faints away—selah!

5 You have seized hold of the lids that guard my eyes—
I am too disturbed to speak!

6 I have considered days from of old,
Years from eternities ago.

7 In the night I will call to mind my song,
I will speak with my heart, and my spirit will inquire.

8 Will Adonai reject us for eternity,
No more to look with favor, ever?

9 Is God's covenantal love gone for all time,
God's speech finished for every generation?

10 Has God forgotten how to offer grace?
Have You in anger shut off the compassion of Your womb?

11 For I said: "I am weak with this—
The changing of the right hand of the Most High."

12 I will call to mind the deeds of Yah,
Yes, let me call to mind Your wonders from of old.

13 I will meditate on all Your workings,
And I will speak about Your deeds:

14 God, Your path is in holiness.
   Who is a great god like God?
15 **You are the Doing-Wonders God,**
   You have made known to the peoples Your strength.
16 With Your arm You have redeemed Your people,
   The children of Jacob and Joseph—selah!
17 The waters saw You, God;
   The waters saw You and roiled,
   Even the angry deeps were raging!
18 Dark clouds stormed with water,
   The skies gave forth their voice,
   Your lightning-arrows shot this way and that.
19 The voice of Your thunder was in the whirlwind,
   Lightnings flashed around the world,
   The earth raged and shook.
20 Your way was in the sea,
   Your paths in churning waters;
   But Your footsteps were not known.
21 You led Your people like the flock
   By the hand of Moses and Aaron.

   ▶ See also Psalms 4 and 118.

Before Traveling
PSALM 138

In this time of excitement and anticipation before travel, we pray for safety and to be able to experience this time in a different location with presence of body, mind, and spirit. May we embrace this opportunity for learning and growth with humility, so that each new experience opens us to the wisdom and beauty of the unknown.

1 Of David.
  I will give thanks to You with all my heart—
  Before magistrates mighty as gods, it is to You I will sing.
2 I will fall prostrate before Your holy palace
  And I will give praise to Your name,
  For Your covenantal love and for Your truth,
  For You have enlarged Your speech beyond even Your name.
3 **In the day I called—You answered me,**
  You broaden the strength of my being.
4 All the sovereigns of the earth shall praise You,
  For they have heard the words of Your mouth;
5 And they shall sing of the ways of Adonai,
  For the glory of Adonai is large indeed.
6 Adonai is raised high, yet God regards the lowly—
  But the high and mighty God knows from a distance.
7 If I walk amidst trouble, You will preserve my life;
  Against the anger of my enemies You send forth Your hand,
  And Your right hand delivers me.
8 Adonai makes things happen for me,
  Adonai, Your covenantal love is eternal—
  Do not abandon the works of Your hands.

▶ See also Psalm 24; for travel to Israel, see Psalm 126.

הִנֵּה מַה־טּוֹב וּמַה־נָּעִים שֶׁבֶת אַחִים גַּם־יָחַד:

A Long-Anticipated Meeting

PSALM 133

The words of the opening line of Psalm 133 remind us of the very beginning of Creation when we learn that human beings are not meant to be alone. As we navigate the anxiety, expectations, and excitement of meeting, we pray for open hearts and the ability to forge new connections and relationships with courage, understanding, and patience.

1 A Song of Ascendings. Of David.
  Behold how good and how pleasant
  Is the dwelling of family all together!
2 Like good oil upon the head
  Running down upon the beard, Aaron's beard,
  That runs down upon the mouth of his garments;
3 Like the dew of Hermon that runs down upon the hills of Zion,
  For there God commanded the blessing—
  Life, till eternity.

▶ See also Psalms 117 and 147.

Praying for the Growth of an Embryo

PSALM 37

*This is a moment of possibility and precariousness, so near to the fulfill-
ment of a deep longing. Psalm 37 speaks of inheritance and dwelling in
the land forever. As we meditate on the many meanings of dwelling and
inheritance, we pray that our anxieties will be calmed and that these words
will be a source of hope, confidence, strength, and faith that our yearnings
are heard.*

1 Of David.
   Avoid getting fired up because of those who feed on evil
   And do not seethe with envy at those who act wickedly—
2 For like grass they will soon be cut down,
   They will wither like green herbs.
3 Believe in Adonai and do good;
   Dwell in the land and feed on faith.
4 Fill yourself with joy over Adonai,
   Who will grant you the petitions of your heart.
5 Cast your path before Adonai;
   Trust in God, and the Holy One will act.
6 God will bring forth justice for you like light
   And judgments in your favor will shine like the brightness
      of noon.
7 Devote yourself to Adonai, wait longingly for God.
   Do not get fired up against the one whose path prospers,
   Against the one who does wicked things.
8 Erase wrath and forsake fury,
   Do not get fired up only to do evil.
9 For evildoers shall be cut off—
   But those who wait hopefully for God? They shall inherit
      the earth.
10 For in a little while, the wicked one is gone—
   Look carefully at her place and she is gone.

11 For the humble shall inherit the earth
   And fill themselves with joy at the abundance of peace.
12 Greedy wicked people plot against the just
   And gnash their teeth against them.
13 Adonai laughs at the wicked,
   Seeing that their day is coming.
14 Heinous folk have unsheathed their sword and bent their bow
   To fell the poor and the needy
   And slaughter those on an upright path.
15 Their sword will enter their own heart,
   And their bows shall be shattered!
16 Indeed, better the little that belongs to the just person
   Than the abundance that belongs to a multitude of wicked.
17 For the arms of the wicked shall be broken
   While Adonai upholds the just.
18 Just Ruler Adonai knows the days of the unblemished:
   Their inheritance shall be eternal.
19 They shall not be ashamed in an evil time,
   And in days of famine they shall be satiated.
20 Know that the wicked shall perish,
   And that the enemies of Adonai, like the fat of lambs,
   Are consumed in smoke—consumed!
21 Lo, a wicked person posts a loan and does not repay,
   While the just person acts graciously and gives.
22 Let those whom God has blessed inherit land,
   While those cursed by the Holy One will be cut off.
23 Humanity's steps have their foundation from Adonai;
   God delights in each one's path—
24 Should they fall, they are not hurled down,
   For Adonai supports their hand.
25 Not in my youth nor in my old age
   Have I seen a just person abandoned
   Or their seed searching for bread;
26 All day long they act graciously and lend,
   And their seed becomes a blessing.
27 Oh turn from evildoing; rather—do good
   And dwell till time everlasting.

28 For Adonai loves justice
And will not abandon the members of the covenant—
They are protected forever,
But the seed of the wicked is cut off.

29 Just people shall inherit the land
And they shall dwell forever upon it.

30 Quietly the mouth of the just meditates on wisdom
And their tongue utters judgment.

31 **The Torah of their God is in their heart;**
Their steps will not totter.

32 Ruthless people look on a just person
And seek to kill him;

33 Adonai will not abandon him in that one's hand,
Nor let him be condemned when he is judged.

34 Steadfastly hope in Adonai and keep God's way
And the Eternal will raise you up to inherit the land;
When the wicked are cut off, you will see.

35 Too often have I watched the wicked be ruthless,
Spreading out like a native plant, its leaves luxuriant.

36 Then he passes by and behold! he is no more,
Though I searched for him, I found him not.

37 Uplift the innocent person,
Mark the upright,
For there is a future for a peaceful person.

38 But the wicked shall be wiped out together—
The future of the wicked is cut off.

39 Victory for the just is from Adonai,
Their stronghold in time of trouble.

40 Adonai will help them and rescue them,
God rescues them from the vicious with victory,
For they have taken refuge in God.

► See also Psalm 139.

אֱלֹהִים שִׁיר חָדָשׁ אָשִׁירָה לָּךְ

Beginning a Process of Expanding One's Family
PSALM 144

Psalm 144 speaks of God's partnership and of a hopeful future in which we will be able to share the love and care we long to provide. We pray for perseverance, comfort, support, and partnership with You as we navigate the disappointments and hopes of this process.

1 Of David.
   Praised be Adonai my Rock,
   Who trains my hands for the battle,
   My fingers for the war.

2 Source of my covenantal love and my fortress,
   My stronghold and the One in whom I take refuge,
   My shield and the One in whom I take shelter,
   Who subdues my people under me.

3 Adonai, what is a person that You should know about her;
   A child, that You should think about him!

4 Human beings are like a vapor,
   Their days like a passing shadow.

5 Adonai, bend down Your heavens and descend,
   Touch the mountains that they smoke;

6 Ignite the lightning and scatter the enemies,
   Send forth Your arrows that they grow confused,

7 Send forth Your hand from on high,
   Set me free, deliver me, from the deluge of the deep,
   From the hand of foreigners

8 Whose mouths have spoken falsehood,
   Whose right hand is the right hand of mendacity.

9 **O God, a new song I would sing to You;**
   On a lute of ten strings I would play melodies for You—

10 Who gives deliverance to monarchs,
    Who frees David, divine servant,
    From the evil sword.

11 Set me free! Deliver me from the hand of foreigners,
Whose mouths have spoken falsehood,
Whose right hand is the right hand of mendacity.

12 We whose sons are like plants grown up even in their youth,
Whose daughters are like corners hewn in the structure of
a palace—

13 Our granaries are full, feed flowing over feed;
Our flocks multiply by the thousands, by the ten-thousands
In our open pastures;

14 Our domestic animals are laden;
There is no breach of our walls, no untoward exodus,
And no outcry in our streets—

15 Happy the people who has it thus,
Happy the people whose God is Adonai.

▶ See also Psalm 139.

Psalms for Commemoration

Sometimes, the flow of time feels like water. We are leaves, carried away with the stream, changing, unfolding, and aging while doing little else than breathing in and breathing out, watching the flow of time. Yet water, like loss, can also overwhelm us or weigh us down. We carry the weight of grief in our hearts and bodies. We look for words to commemorate what is lost forever.

וְאַתָּה יְיָ מָגֵן בַּעֲדִי

Shivah—The Week After Losing a Beloved

PSALM 3

At this time of often overwhelming grief and shock, this psalm reminds us of God's protection and loving presence, even when it is difficult to perceive. We pray for continued faith, strength, and hope as we mourn.

1 A psalm of David
When he fled from the face of Absalom,
His son.

2 Adonai, how many are my adversaries!
So many rise up against me!

3 So many say about me:
"There is no deliverance for *him* in God—
Selah!"

4 **But You, Adonai, are a shield for me,**
My glory,
The One who lifts up my head.

5 My voice cries out to Adonai
Who will respond to me from God's holy mountain—
Selah!

6 *Now I lay me down to sleep—*
And then I will awake, for Adonai upholds me.

7 I shall not fear the thousands
Who have set themselves against me, all around:

8 Arise, Adonai! Deliver me, my God!
You have smitten every one of my enemies on the cheek,
You have broken the teeth of the terrible ones!

9 Deliverance belongs to God,
Your blessing is upon Your people—
Selah!

▶ See also Psalms 16 and 103.

Sh'loshim—The Month After Losing a Beloved
PSALM 13

As we continue to wade in our mourning and navigate a new reality without our beloved, we look for solace in God's steadfast love. This psalm invites us to pour out our hearts knowing that God is with us in our pain and brokenness.

1 For the conductor: A psalm of David.

2 How long, Adonai?!
Will You forget me forever?
How long will You keep hiding Your face from me?

3 How long will I keep taking counsel alone,
With anguish in my heart all day?
How long will my enemies rise up over me?

4 Look down—
Respond to me, Adonai my God!
Restore light to my eyes—
Lest I sleep with death,

5 Lest my enemy say, "I have overpowered this one!"
Lest my oppressors rejoice when I stumble.

6 As for me,
In Your covenantal love I trust;
My heart rejoices in Your victories.
I will sing to Adonai,
How You have splashed me with Your love.

▶ See also Psalms 33, 77, and 131.

כִּי מַלְאָכָיו יְצַוֶּה־לָּךְ לִשְׁמָרְךָ בְּכָל־דְּרָכֶיךָ:

At the Grave of a Beloved

PSALM 91

As we stand at this place of memory, the words of Psalm 91 embrace us with compassion and solace. Although we do not know what comes after this life, we seek reassurance that our beloved is protected, loved, and at peace.

1 One who dwells in the hidden place of the Most High,
Who spends the night in the shade of Shaddai:

2 I say to Adonai, my refuge and my stronghold,
My God:
I trust in You,

3 For the Holy One will save you from the trap of the hunter,
From the ruinous plague.

4 Like branches on a sukkah
God will cover you with outstretched pinions,
And beneath holy wings
Will be your refuge.
God's truth is our shield and buckler,

5 So do not be afraid of the terror of the night,
Of arrows flying by in daytime,

6 Of the plague that stalks in darkness
Or the horror that ravages at noon.

7 A thousand may fall at your side,
Ten thousand on your right hand—
Nothing shall touch you.

8 Only look with your eyes,
And see the payback of the wicked!

9 For You, Adonai, are my refuge;
And when you, my friend, make the Most High
Your dwelling-place,

10 No harm will happen to you,
No calamity will draw near to your tent.

11 **For God will command the angels to you,**
To guard you in all your ways;

12 They shall carry you upon their hands
   Lest your foot be struck with a stone.
13 You can walk amid cubs and vipers,
   You can trample fierce lions and snakes.
14 God says:
   "Because you are devoted to Me I will rescue you,
   I will protect you, for you know My name.
15 Call to Me and I shall come;
   I am with you in trouble,
   I will deliver you and I will honor you.
16 I will satisfy you with length of days—long days;
   I will let you see the proof
   Of My deliverance."

   ▶ See also Psalm 23.

עָשָׂה יָרֵחַ לְמוֹעֲדִים

Unveiling

PSALM 104

An unveiling is a time of boundaries: boundaries between recent loss and the loss we experienced a year ago, boundaries between a place of burial and a place of memory. Psalm 104 reminds us—even with these boundaries—of the interconnectedness of all creation and the divine presence in all aspects of life . . . including death.

1 Praise Adonai, O my being,
   Adonai my God, You are grand indeed!
   You are clothed in surpassing splendor—
2 Wrapping Yourself in light like a cloak,
   Unwrapping the heavens like a curtain of smoke,
3 Laying the beams of Your upper chambers in the waters,
   Turning clouds into Your chariot,
   Walking about on the wings of the wind,
4 Making the winds Your messengers;
   Flaming fire, Your ministers.
5 You have established earth on her foundations—
   It shall not totter, to infinity and beyond.
6 You covered it with the deep like a mantle—
   The waters stood up on the mountains.
7 They ran away from Your rebuke,
   They hurried off from the sound of Your thunder.
8 Mountains rose up, valleys dropped down
   To the very place You had established for them.
9 You set up a boundary they could not cross,
   So they could not roar back to deluge the earth.
10 You are the One who sends forth streams into the river valleys
   That meander among the mountains;
11 They give water to every beast of the field;
   The wild donkeys quench their thirst.
12 Above them hover the heavenly flocks,
   From among the foliage they send forth their voice.

13 You water the hills from Your upper chamber;
   From the fruit of Your works the earth is satisfied.
14 You make grass sprout up for the cattle,
   Herbage for the work of the human world
   To bring forth bread from the earth,
15 Wine that rejoices the human heart,
   Making the face glow brighter than oil,
   And bread—sustaining the human heart.
16 The trees of Adonai drink their fill,
   The cedars of Lebanon which God has planted,
17 Where birds build nests:
   The stork's house is in the fir trees.
18 The crags are for the mountain goats,
   The rocks are a refuge for rabbits.
19 **God made a moon for seasons;**
   The sun knows the time to go in.
20 You decree darkness—and it is night,
   When all the creatures of the forest crawl about,
21 The young lions roar for their nourishment,
   And seek their food from God.
22 The sun rises—they withdraw,
   And spread out in their lairs.
23 People go forth to their work,
   To their labor, until evening.
24 How many are Your works, Adonai!
   All of them You made with wisdom!
   The earth is full of Your creatures.
25 This is the sea—great and many hands wide!
   There—creeping things without number,
   Wild things, little ones and big ones.
26 There go the ships,
   And a writhing monster, this creature You formed to play in
      the sea—
27 All of them wait for You
   To give them their food in its time.
28 You give to them, they go gathering,
   You open Your hand—they are given good aplenty.

13 You water the hills from Your upper chamber;
From the fruit of Your works the earth is satisfied.
14 You make grass sprout up for the cattle,
Herbage for the work of the human world
To bring forth bread from the earth,
15 Wine that rejoices the human heart,
Making the face glow brighter than oil,
And bread—sustaining the human heart.
16 The trees of Adonai drink their fill,
The cedars of Lebanon which God has planted,
17 Where birds build nests:
The stork's house is in the fir trees.
18 The crags are for the mountain goats,
The rocks are a refuge for rabbits.
19 **God made a moon for seasons;**
The sun knows the time to go in.
20 You decree darkness—and it is night,
When all the creatures of the forest crawl about,
21 The young lions roar for their nourishment,
And seek their food from God.
22 The sun rises—they withdraw,
And spread out in their lairs.
23 People go forth to their work,
To their labor, until evening.
24 How many are Your works, Adonai!
All of them You made with wisdom!
The earth is full of Your creatures.
25 This is the sea—great and many hands wide!
There—creeping things without number,
Wild things, little ones and big ones.
26 There go the ships,
And a writhing monster, this creature You formed to play in
the sea—
27 All of them wait for You
To give them their food in its time.
28 You give to them, they go gathering,
You open Your hand—they are given good aplenty.

עָשָׂה יָרֵחַ לְמוֹעֲדִים

Unveiling

PSALM 104

*An unveiling is a time of boundaries: boundaries between recent loss and
the loss we experienced a year ago, boundaries between a place of burial
and a place of memory. Psalm 104 reminds us—even with these boundaries—of the interconnectedness of all creation and the divine presence in all
aspects of life . . . including death.*

1 Praise Adonai, O my being,
 Adonai my God, You are grand indeed!
 You are clothed in surpassing splendor—
2 Wrapping Yourself in light like a cloak,
 Unwrapping the heavens like a curtain of smoke,
3 Laying the beams of Your upper chambers in the waters,
 Turning clouds into Your chariot,
 Walking about on the wings of the wind,
4 Making the winds Your messengers;
 Flaming fire, Your ministers.
5 You have established earth on her foundations—
 It shall not totter, to infinity and beyond.
6 You covered it with the deep like a mantle—
 The waters stood up on the mountains.
7 They ran away from Your rebuke,
 They hurried off from the sound of Your thunder.
8 Mountains rose up, valleys dropped down
 To the very place You had established for them.
9 You set up a boundary they could not cross,
 So they could not roar back to deluge the earth.
10 You are the One who sends forth streams into the river valleys
 That meander among the mountains;
11 They give water to every beast of the field;
 The wild donkeys quench their thirst.
12 Above them hover the heavenly flocks,
 From among the foliage they send forth their voice.

עֶזְרִי מֵעִם יְיָ עֹשֵׂה שָׁמַיִם וָאָרֶץ:

Yahrzeit—A Year After Losing a Beloved
PSALM 121

A text from the Jerusalem Talmud, Sanhedrin 10:2, tells a story of King David digging the foundation of the Temple when he hits a clay pot that is holding back the abyss. When David moves the pot, the land becomes flooded by darkness; only by singing psalms—including Psalm 121—can he lift the world from the abyss. Reaching the yahrzeit of a loved one, we are like the clay pot standing between darkness and hope, and like David, singing a song of wholeness.

1 A Song of Ascendings:
  I will raise my eyes to the mountains:
  From where will come my help?

2 **My help is from the realm of Adonai,**
  Maker of heaven and earth.

3 God will not allow your foot to slip:
  Your Guardian will not doze;

4 Behold, the Guardian of Israel
  Does not doze and does not sleep.

5 Adonai is your Guardian,
  Adonai is Your shade over Your right hand.

6 By day the sun shall not smite you,
  Nor the moon at night.

7 Adonai will stand sentry, guarding you from all harm—
  Guarding your very life.

8 Adonai will stand sentry over your going out and your coming in
  From now until eternity.

▶ See also Psalms 33 and 119.

29 You hide Your face, they are terrified,
   You cut off their breath—they perish,
   And to their dust they return.
30 You send forth Your breath, they are created anew
   And You renew the face of the ground.
31 Let the glory of Adonai last forever,
   Let Adonai rejoice in divine works,
32 Who looks upon the earth and it trembles,
   Who touches the mountains and they smoke.
33 Let me sing to Adonai during my lifetime,
   Let me sing praise to God while I still am!
34 Let my meditation rest sweetly upon the Holy One—
   I will rejoice in Adonai!
35 Let sinners cease from the earth
   And wicked people be no more;
   Praise Adonai, O my being,
   Hall'lu-Yah, Praise Adonai!

▶ See also Psalm 126.

אִם־לֹא שִׁוִּיתִי וְדוֹמַמְתִּי

Remembering a Life-Changing Loss
PSALM 131

This loss is an integral part of our life's journey; it is always with us. Sometimes this loss is at the forefront of our thoughts, loud and painful. Other times it dwells quietly in the back of our minds.

1 A Song of Ascendings. Of David.
Adonai, my heart is not haughty
And my eyes are not raised up in scorn,
Nor do I take my place among great things
Or things too wondrous for me.

2 **I affirm that I have quietly composed myself;**
Like a weaned child upon its mother—
Like a weaned child is my desire.

3 Let Israel wait for Adonai
From now until forever!

▶ See also Psalms 6, 31, and 122.

שָׁם יָשַׁבְנוּ גַּם־בָּכִינוּ

Remembering a Traumatic Event

PSALM 137

This psalm evokes the sorrow of Tishah B'Av and the destruction of the Temple. The words of sorrow and pain link us to the despair our ancestors felt, reminding us that even when we return to our darkest moments, we are never alone.

1 On the riverbanks of Babel
There we sat; we sobbed, as well,
When Zion came to mind.

2 On the willows in her midst
We hanged our lyres,

3 For there our jailers cajoled us: Join in song!
And our haranguers asked for jollity:
Join in jolly songs of Zion!

4 How shall we join in jolly song to Adonai
On foreign soil?!

5 "Jerusalem, if I jettison my memory of you,
Let my right hand jettison her strength,

6 Let my tongue cling to my jowl—
If I cast you from my mind,
If I do not raise up Jerusalem
Above the juncture of my joys." . . .

▶ See also Psalms 31 and 147.

יִסְתְּרֵנִי בְּסֵתֶר אָהֳלוֹ בְּצוּר יְרוֹמְמֵנִי:

Choosing to End a Pregnancy

PSALM 27

We look for comfort and assurance in our hearts as we navigate the complex emotions of choosing to end a pregnancy. May we sense protection, safety, and security in God's loving embrace. May our hearts be filled with peace, knowing that we are not alone and that God's grace is unconditional.

1 Of David.
  Adonai is my light and my victory—
  From whom should I feel fright?
  Adonai is the stronghold of my life—
  From whom should I feel terror?

2 When evildoers approach me in battle to feed on my flesh—
  My pursuers, my adversaries—
  They have stumbled, they have fallen down.

3 If a camp encamps against me, my heart will not fear;
  If a war arises against me,
  In this I would trust:

4 One thing have I sought from Adonai—how I long for it:
  That I may live in the House of Adonai all the days of my life;
  That I may look upon the sweetness of Adonai,
  And spend time in the Palace;

5 That You might hide me in Your sukkah on a chaotic day,
  Hide me in the hiding places of Your tent,
  Raise me high upon a rock.

6 Now my head rises high above my enemies roundabout,
  And in Your tent I'll offer offerings to the sound of *t'ruah*.
  I shall sing and chant praises to Adonai!

7 Hear, Adonai, my voice—
  I am crying out!
  Be gracious to me, answer me!

8 My heart has said to You: "Seek my face."
  I am seeking Your face, Adonai—

9 Do not hide Your face from me.
   Do not turn Your servant away in anger,
   You have been my help—
   Do not forsake me, do not abandon me, God of my deliverance!
10 For my father and my mother have abandoned me,
   Yet Adonai gathers me up.
11 Make Your path apparent to me,
   Guide me in the upright road
   Because of those up ahead who lie in wait for me.
12 Do not hand me over to the lust of my adversaries—
   For false witnesses have risen against me,
   Fuming violently!
13 Had I not the faith
   That I would see the goodness of God in the land of life . . .
14 Wait for Adonai—
   Fill your waiting with hope in Adonai;
   Let your heart be strong and of good courage,
   And wait hopefully for Adonai.

▶ See also Psalm 46.

כִּי גָבַר עָלֵינוּ חַסְדּוֹ

Anniversaries

PSALM 117

Whether marking this day in celebration or solemnity, we are aware of the passing of time and grateful to be present in this moment. This psalm holds us in times of joy and times of commemoration.

1 Sing *Hallel* to Adonai, all peoples—
Praise God, all nations!
2 **For God's covenantal love empowers us,**
The Eternal's truth immortalizes us,
Hall'lu-Yah!

▶ See also Psalm 100.

וַיִּתְהַלְכוּ מִגּוֹי אֶל־גּוֹי

Marking Time Since or Leading to Moving

PSALM 105

During our own moments of leaving, this psalm connects us with the foundational narrative of our people's Exodus from Egypt.

1 Give thanks to Adonai, call out the Name,
   Demonstrate God's deeds among the people!

2 Sing to God, make music,
   Meditate on all God's wondrous acts!

3 Praise together the Holy One's name—
   Let the heart of those who reach for Adonai rejoice!

4 Search out Adonai, search out God's strength,
   Seek the divine face continually;

5 Remember the wondrous acts the Eternal has done,
   The marvelous things and the judgments of God's mouth!

6 O seed of Abraham, God's servant—
   O children of Jacob, God's chosen one—

7 Adonai is our God;
   Divine judgments are in all the earth.

8 The Holy One has forever kept the covenant in mind
   (A word commanded to a thousand generations)

9 First cut with Abraham,
   Then sworn as an oath to Isaac,

10 God set it up for an unbreakable law for Jacob,
   An eternal covenant for Israel,

11 Saying, "To you I tender the Territory of Canaan,
   The portion of your inheritance,"

12 When they were few in number,
   A scattering, strangers in the land.

13 **When they went about from nation to nation,**
   From one realm to another people,

14 God did not let anyone harm them,
   Rebuking monarchs on their behalf:

15 "Do not touch My anointed one
    And to My prophets do no harm!"

16 When God foretold a famine in the land,
    Smashing every staff of bread,

17 The Holy One sent a man before them:
    Joseph was sold for a slave;

18 They afflicted his feet with fetters,
    His body they put in irons.

19 Until the time his prediction came about,
    The word of Adonai tested him.

20 The king sent forth and unbound him,
    The ruler of peoples let him go;

21 He set him as lord of his house
    And ruler over all his possessions,

22 To bind his princes to him
    And to give his elders wisdom.

23 Then Israel came into oppressive Egypt
    And Jacob sojourned in the land of Cham.

24 God made the people very fruitful,
    Stronger than their oppressors.

25 But God turned their hearts to hate the people,
    To despise God's servants.

26 The Holy One sent Moses, servant of the Divine,
    Aaron, whom God had chosen,

27 And gave them the words of God's signs,
    To all the wonders of the Holy One in the land of Cham.

28 The Eternal sent darkness, and it darkened—
    The plagues did not rebel against Your word.

29 You turned their waters into blood,
    And killed their fish.

30 Their land swarmed with frogs—
    Amid the very chambers of their rulers!

31 You spoke—and a swarm arrived:
    Lice in all their borders.

32 You turned their rains into hail,
    Flaming fire in their land;

33 You smote their vineyards and fig trees
   And smashed the trees on their borders.
34 You spoke—and the locusts arrived,
   Cicadas without number,
35 Which ate up all the herbage of their land,
   And ate up the fruit of their ground.
36 And You smote all the firstborn of their land,
   First-fruits of all their vigor.
37 And You brought the Israelites out with silver and gold,
   And no one tottered among the tribes.
38 The Egyptians rejoiced when they withdrew,
   For fear of them had fallen upon them.
39 You spread a cloud for a screen,
   And fire to light up the night.
40 The people queried, and You brought quail,
   With bread from the skies You sated them;
41 You opened a rock, and waters gushed forth,
   They ran—a river in the desert!
42 Thus God kept in mind the holy word
   With Abraham, God's servant,
43 And brought forth the people with joy,
   The chosen ones with singing.
44 You gave the lands of the nations to them,
   And they would take possession of the labor of the peoples—
45 That they might keep Your statutes
   And guard Your laws.
   Hall'lu-Yah!

► See also Psalms 122 and 138.

Psalms for Despair

Sometimes we move through our lives like we travel a road. Consciously we set each foot in front of the other—deliberately pacing our way, creating our life's journey. At other times, we find our paths unnavigable, as the bitterness of loss in our hearts and bodies weighs us down. We look for words, for vessels, for ways to hold the things that are hard to name.

כִּי־טוֹב חַסְדְּךָ מֵחַיִּים שְׂפָתַי יְשַׁבְּחוּנְךָ׃

Accepting Death

PSALM 63

As we accept the reality of life's impermanence, we look to God for courage, assurance, and comfort. We pray for tranquility and peace for our loved ones and ourselves as we work to embrace the transition from this life into God's eternal embrace.

1 A psalm of David, when he was in the wilderness of Judah.
2 You are God—my God;
I seek You at dawn,
The life-breath of me thirsts for You,
The flesh of me grows faint for You
In a dry and weary land, without water.
3 Yes, in holy places I have had visions of You,
Looking upon Your power and Your glory;
4 **Because Your covenantal love is better than life**
My lips shape words of praise for You.
5 Yes, I will bless You throughout my life;
I will raise my palms in psalms to Your name!
6 My being is sated, as though I were fed the most succulent meal,
And my mouth praises You with song on my lips
7 When I evoke Your presence upon my bed,
And meditate upon You through the watches of the night.
8 For You have been a help to me,
And in the shade of Your wings I shall sing praise.
9 My being clings to You—it would run after You
That Your right hand might hold me up.
10 *Yet those who long to liquidate my life*
Shall enter the netherparts of the earth—
11 *They shall be hurled against the power of the sword,*
Dished out as a portion for foxes.
12 But the monarch shall rejoice in God,
All who swear an oath to him shall be praised;
Though the mouth of those who speak lies shall be muzzled.

▶ See also Psalm 62.

גַּם כִּי־אֵלֵךְ בְּגֵיא צַלְמָוֶת לֹא־אִירָא רָע כִּי־אַתָּה עִמָּדִי

The Day After Losing a Beloved

PSALM 23

As our hearts ache with grief, perhaps not yet fully comprehending the depth of our loss, this familiar psalm speaks of God's faithful shepherding and comforting presence. We pray for light in the midst of deep darkness.

1 A psalm of David.
   Adonai, my shepherd:
   I lack for nothing—
2 In meadows thick with grass You lay me down,
   Across streams serene You guide me.
3 My life You restore,
   Leading me serenely in well-worn paths of justice
   To glorify Your name.
4 **Even when I walk in a valley dark as death's shadow**
   I shall fear no evil,
   For You are with me,
   Your staff and Your walking stick—they reassure me.
5 You set a table before me along with my enemies,
   You rain rich oils 'round my head;
   My cup? Overflowing!
6 For certain, goodness and the love of Your covenant
   Will run after me all the days of my life,
   And I shall abide in God's house
   For long days,
   Long, long days.

▶ See also Psalms 3, 61, and 103.

מִקְצֵה הָאָרֶץ אֵלֶיךָ אֶקְרָא

Experiencing a Significant Loss
for the First Time

PSALM 61

Losing a close loved one, particularly for the first time, opens so many questions. The uncertainty of what comes after death can be challenging and comforting, and we wonder what of us is lost with our loved one and what of them remains with us forever. With Psalm 61, we pray for God's comfort, assurance, and closeness in our grief, that our loved one who is no longer physically with us will continue to live on in our lives.

1 For the conductor: on strings.

2 Hear, God, my cry, attend to my prayer!

3 **From the end of the earth echoes my call to You**
When my heart is ebbing—
Lead me to a rock that towers above me!

4 For You have become my refuge,
A tower of strength in the face of the enemy.

5 I shall sojourn in Your tent for eternities,
I shall take refuge in the secret places of Your wings—selah!

6 For You, God, have hearkened to my vows.
You have given me the inheritance of those who revere Your name.

7 May You add seasons to the sovereign's seasons,
May their years be like generation upon generation.

8 May they sit enthroned before God forever—
Appoint mercy and truth to guard them.

9 Thus will I sing Your name forever,
That I may fulfill my vows in every season.

▶ See also Psalms 23 and 73.

אַךְ לֵאלֹהִים דֹּמִּי נַפְשִׁי כִּי־מִמֶּנּוּ תִּקְוָתִי:

Mourning Multiple Losses
PSALM 62

When our hearts feel heavy with memories, Psalm 62 invites us to find solace and wisdom in God's loving embrace. Each loss is unique, and we pray for guidance as we navigate our ocean of solitude, strength to honor the legacies of those who have gone before us, and protection as we find our way forward, even in loneliness.

1 For the conductor: on *Y'dutun*, a psalm
of David.
2 My being is wrapped in silent waiting,
Only for God
From whom comes my deliverance.
3 Only God
Is my rock and my deliverance,
My high tower—
I shall not stumble about.
4 How long will you gang up on someone
That you may commit murder, all of you,
Like a leaning wall, a fence pushed over?
5 Only—they plot to push her from her height.
They delight in lying,
With the mouth they bless and with their innards
they curse—selah!
6 **Wait silently, my being,**
Only for God
From whom comes my hope.

7 Only God
  Is my rock and my deliverance,
  My high tower—
  I shall not stumble.
8 Upon God is my deliverance and my honor,
  The rock of my strength, my refuge, is in God.
9 Trust in God in every period, people;
  Pour out your heart before the Holy One,
  God is a refuge for us—selah!
10 Only vapor
  Are the ordinary people,
  Nobles are a lie;
  When they go up on the scales
  Together they are less than vapor.
11 Do not trust in oppression,
  And in thievery put no false hopes;
  If wealth bears fruit, do not set your heart on it.
12 One thing did God speak,
  Twice have I heard this:
  That strength is with God,
13 And with You, Adonai, is covenantal love—
  For You repay each person according to their deeds.

▶ See also Psalms 23 and 18.

מִמַּעֲמַקִּים קְרָאתִיךָ יְיָ:

When We Fail

PSALM 130

Even as we struggle to forgive ourselves for our errors and failures, we pray to be reminded that our shortcomings do not define us. May we continue to grow with open hearts.

1 A Song of Ascendings.
From the deepest place in me I called You, Adonai.

2 Adonai, listen as my voice ascends!
Let Your ears incline
To the voice of my petition!

3 If You, Yah, were to stand sentry over crooked acts,
Adonai, who would endure?

4 For with You pardon dwells,
That You may be revered.

5 I hoped, Adonai—my whole being hoped,
For God's word have I been waiting.

6 My being yearns for Adonai
More than watchers yearn for the morning—
Watchers for the morning!

7 Let Israel wait for Adonai
For with Adonai is covenantal love,
With God is abundant redemption—

8 And the Holy One will redeem Israel
From all its wrongdoings.

▶ See also Psalms 55 and 73.

לֹא־לָנֶצַח יָרִיב וְלֹא לְעוֹלָם יִטּוֹר׃

When Leaving, Separating, or Divorcing
PSALM 103

When a relationship ends, it is a time of heartache, ambiguity, and loss.
We attempt to figure out who we are without a part of our lives that once
seemed so certain. This psalm, familiar from the Days of Awe, reminds us
of the transience of life and also of life's compassion and grace, which, we
pray, will lead us to wholeness again.

1 Of David.
   Praise Adonai, O my being—
   With everything in me, I bless God's holy name.
2 Praise Adonai, O my being,
   And do not forget all the goodness the Holy One
   has bestowed—
3 Offering forgiveness for all your iniquity,
   Healing for all your illnesses,
4 Redeeming your life from the Pit,
   Crowning you with covenantal love and
   womb-like compassion,
5 Satisfying your middle age with good,
   Renewing your youth like an eagle.
6 Adonai does justice,
   And judgments for all the oppressed.
7 Making known the divine ways to Moses,
   God's doings to the children of Israel.
8 Womb-gentle, gracious, is Adonai,
   Slow to anger and great in covenantal love;
9 **The Holy One will not strive forever,**
   Nor bear a grudge until eternity.
10 God has not dealt with us according to our sins,
   Nor bestowed on us the consequences of our iniquities.
11 For as high as the heavens are above the earth,
   So powerful is God's covenantal love over those who revere
      God's name.

12 As distant as the east is from the west
So has God distanced our rebelliousness from us.

13 As a father shows compassion to his children,
So Adonai embraces with the compassion of the womb those
who revere the Divine.

14 For the Eternal is familiar with our form,
That we are dust is ever in God's mind.

15 The days of a mortal are like grass,
Like a flower of the field she flourishes;

16 When a breeze passes over it, it is no more,
And its place will recognize it no longer.

17 But the covenantal love of Adonai is from everlasting to
everlasting for those who hold the Holy One in awe,
And God's justice is for the children of those who are children
today—

18 For those who keep the covenant,
And those who remain mindful of God's ordinances, that they
may fulfill them.

19 Adonai established the Throne in the heavens,
And God's royalty rules over all.

20 Praise Adonai, divine angels,
Mighty in strength, who do God's word,
Hearkening to the sound of that word;

21 Praise Adonai, all the hosts,
Ministers of the Eternal, doing God's will;

22 Praise Adonai, all God's creatures,
In all the places of the holy realm,
Praise Adonai, O my being!

▶ See also Psalm 147.

חָנֵּנִי יְיָ כִּי צַר־לִי עָשְׁשָׁה בְכַעַס עֵינִי נַפְשִׁי וּבִטְנִי:

After Losing a Wanted Pregnancy

PSALM 31

This is a moment of overwhelming grief and sorrow, the loss of the future we imagined and for which we began to prepare. When others may not fully recognize the depth of our loss, this psalm speaks of God's closeness to us as a refuge and protector.

1 For the conductor,
   A psalm of David.

2 In You, Adonai, have I taken shelter—
   Spare me from unending shame;
   Through Your justice, rescue me.

3 Bend Your ear to me—
   Quickly, save me!
   Be a rock stronghold for me,
   Make my house a fortress, to deliver me.

4 For You are my rock and my fortress,
   And for the sake of Your name, lead me, guide me,

5 Bring me out of this net they have hidden away for me
   For You are my stronghold!

6 Into Your hand I entrust my spirit—
   You've paid my ransom, Adonai, God of truth.

7 I hate those who store up vaporous falsehoods,
   But I—in Adonai have I trusted.

8 I delight, I rejoice in Your covenantal love,
   For You have seen my affliction,
   You know intimately the sufferings of my life.

9 You have not shut me up in the enemy's hand—
   You have stood my legs up on the broad boulevard.

10 **Show grace to me, Adonai, for I am sorely confined,**
   My eye has wasted away in anger, my whole being, my
   whole body!

11 My life has been consumed in agony,
   My years in groaning;
   Through my sin my strength has ebbed,
   My bones are wasting away!
12 Because of all my oppressors I have become a reproach—
   Greatly so, to my neighbors—and a fright to those who know me.
   Those who see me outside run away from me!
13 I am forgotten, like a person dead to the mind,
   I am like a lost vessel.
14 I heard the whispers of many—
   Terror all around!
   When they took counsel together against me,
   They plotted to take my life.
15 But I, I trusted in You, Adonai,
   I said: "You are my God!"
16 My times are in Your hand—
   Deliver me from the hand of my enemies, my pursuers;
17 Light up Your face before Your servant,
   Make me victorious through Your covenantal love.
18 Adonai, let me not be shamed, for I have called out to You;
   Let the wicked be shamed, let them be silenced in Sheol.
19 Let the lying lips be dumb
   Of those who speak in arrogance against the just—
   In pride and contempt!
20 How great is Your goodness, which You have stored away for
      those who revere You;
   You have labored for those who take refuge in You from others.
21 You have secreted them in the secret places of Your presence,
   Away from unsavory people's plotting;
   You have hidden them in a sukkah away from arguing tongues.
22 Blessed is Adonai
   Who has revealed the wonders of Your covenantal love
   Within the rocky fortress of my city.
23 As for me, I said in my haste,
   "I am cut off from the sight of Your eyes!"
   Still, You heard my voice in prayer
   When I cried out to You.

24 Love Adonai, all who are devoted to God.
   Adonai preserves the faithful,
   But penalizes heavily those who act with pride.
25 Be strong, and let your heart find courage,
   All who wait hopefully for Adonai.

▶ See also Psalms 34 and 147.

קָרוֹב יְיָ לְנִשְׁבְּרֵי־לֵב וְאֶת־דַּכְּאֵי־רוּחַ יוֹשִׁיעַ:

Experiencing Infertility

PSALM 34

As we experience the unique and terrible pain of infertility, its emotional turmoil and ongoing disappointment, we may feel that we are endlessly seeking God, looking for stability when nothing seems to go as planned. In the midst of despair that threatens to crush us, yet goes unseen by so many, we pray for a renewed sense of trust and hope.

1 Of David: When he disguised his tastes before Abimelech—
   who let him go free—and he went on his way.

2 A blessing I will bring to Adonai in every season—
   God's praise is always in my mouth.

3 By my life may Adonai be praised,
   May the humble hear and be happy.

4 Call out the greatness of Adonai with me,
   Let us raise high the Divine Name together!

5 Daily I sought out Adonai—who responded!
   From all my dread You rescued me.

6 Every face that looks to God shall glow,
   No shame shall ever veil it.

7 From this poor man came a cry—Adonai heard,
   And delivered him from all his troubles.

8 God sends a messenger who sets up camp
   Around all who hold the Holy One in awe,
   And rescues them.

9 Have a taste and see how truly good is God—
   Happy the person who takes refuge with Adonai.

10 If you see the awe of God, you can share that holiness,
   And you will lack for nothing in your lives.

11 Juvenile lions lack and lunge, hunting, hungry—
   But those who lean on Adonai lack little that is good.

12 Keep faith, children—come, listen to me
   That I may teach you the awe of Adonai.

13 Learn who the person is who longs for life,
   Who loves days of seeing good:

14 Monitor your tongue, let it speak no evil,
   And your lips—let them murmur no deceit.

15 Negate evildoing; rather, do good—
   Seek peace and harmony—pursue them!

16 On the just do God's eyes rest;
   The ears of Adonai open to their cry.

17 Prepare, O doers of evil, for the anger of God's face,
   Cutting off any remnant of you from the earth.

18 Quaking, the just cried out—and God heard,
   And from all their troubles Adonai rescued them.

19 **Rays of God's presence warm the broken of heart,**
   Adonai will deliver those whose spirits are crushed.

20 Streams of sorrow may burden the just,
   But Adonai is preparing a rescue for all,

21 Tenderly guarding all of their bones—
   Not one of them will be broken.

22 Unrighteousness destroys the unworthy;
   Vilifiers of the just will be condemned as guilty.

23 Wait for God's rescue,
   You servants of Adonai!
   Zeal toward God's refuge will protect you from guilt.

▶ See also Psalms 31 and 130.

Psalms for Gratitude

At times our hearts and souls are full of gratitude. Gratitude is not a passive experience, but the active awareness of the gifts—large and small—that fill our spirits with a sense of abundance, humility, and deep connection. When our hearts are lifted, our words, carried aloft on gentle breezes, resonate in the boundless heavens that cradle our every blessing.

תֶּחִי־נַפְשִׁי וּתְהַלְלֶךָ

Birthdays

PSALM 119

Birthdays are times when we experience a wide range of emotions: joy and gratitude, and perhaps also anxiety for the future or regrets about the past. Psalm 119—our longest psalm—affirms life, and one tradion invites us to return to it year after year, reading the verse that corresponds to our age or the verses that begin with the letters of our names.

1 Always happy are those who are upright in the way,
  Who walk in the Torah of Adonai;

2 Always happy are those who keep Your testimonies,
  Who seek You with all their heart;

3 Avoiding all injustice,
  They walk in Your ways.

4 Adonai, You commanded Your precepts
  To be thoroughly observed.

5 Ah, that my ways might be directed
  To observe Your statutes—

6 After that, I would avoid being ashamed
  When I look at all Your mitzvot,

7 Acknowledging You with an upright heart
  When I learn Your righteous judgments.

8 As I advance the practice of Your statutes,
  Abandon me not—not ever, not ever.

9 By what means shall a young person purify her path?
  By guarding Your word;

10 Bringing my whole heart to seek You out—
  Cause me not to err in Your mitzvot;

11 Binding Your word in the recesses of my heart
  That I might not sin against You.

12 Blessed are You, Adonai—
  Teach me Your statutes.

13 Between my lips I have told
  Tales of all the judgments of Your mouth,

14 Becoming as joyful in the path of Your testimonies
   As over all riches;
15 By Your precepts I will meditate,
   And I will look well to Your ways.
16 Because of Your statutes I will delight;
   I shall not forget Your words.
17 Come, deal bountifully with Your servant that I may live
   And keep Your words.
18 Cause my eyes to open, that I may see
   Wonders out of Your Torah.
19 Cast out as a sojourner in the land am I—
   Do not hide Your mitzvot from me!
20 Crushed am I with longing,
   At every season, for Your judgments.
21 Cursed ones, the haughty, did You rebuke
   For erring in Your mitzvot.
22 Cast off shame and contempt from me,
   For I have guarded Your testimonies.
23 Crowned princes sat and spoke against me,
   Yet Your servant still meditates on Your statutes.
24 Concerning Your testimonies I have taken delight—
   In them do I take counsel.
25 Dust has invaded my being—
   Restore my life, as You have declared.
26 Detailing my ways, I was answered by You;
   Teach me Your statutes.
27 Describe for me the path of Your precepts,
   That I may meditate on Your wonders.
28 Drooped over from grief am I—
   Sustain me according to Your word!
29 Discard for me the path of falsehood;
   Grant me the grace of Your Torah.
30 Deciding for the path of faithfulness am I,
   Setting Your judgments before me.
31 Dearly have I cleaved to Your testimonies;
   Adonai, put me not to shame.
32 Directed to Your mitzvot, I begin to run,

For You have expanded my heart.

33 Educate me, Adonai, in the way of Your statutes,
And I will guard them with every step.

34 Enlighten me, that I may guard Your Torah,
And I will observe it with all my heart.

35 Envelop me in the path of Your mitzvot,
For in it I delight.

36 Extend my heart to be near Your testimonies,
But not near material gain.

37 Enjoin my eyes from seeing falsehood,
Restore my life through Your way.

38 Exalt Your servant with Your word
Which leads to reverence for You.

39 End my shame, which I so fear,
For Your judgments are good.

40 Even is my desire for Your precepts;
Restore my life through Your justice.

41 Favor me with Your covenantal love, Adonai,
Your deliverance, according to Your word;

42 Framing an answer for me to the one whose word would
shame me,
For I have trusted in Your word.

43 From my mouth, I pray, do not remove the entire word of truth,
Since I wait for Your judgment.

44 For I will keep Your Torah always,
Till the end of time,

45 Freely walking about, at ease,
For I have sought Your precepts,

46 Facing monarchs with words of Your testimonies,
Never feeling shame.

47 Feeling delight in Your mitzvot
Which I have loved,

48 Fingers spread, palms lifted, to Your mitzvot,
Which I have loved,
Full of reflective thoughts on Your statutes.

49 Give attention to the word You promised to Your servant,
For You have allowed me hope,

50 Greeting my affliction with Your comfort,
   That Your word might renew my life.
51 Glory-seekers mocked me greatly,
   But I have not turned aside from Your Torah,
52 Grateful, Adonai, for remembering Your judgments from of old
   And I have been comforted.
53 Great fury has seized me, because of wicked people
   Who abandon Your Torah.
54 Gentle serenades Your statutes sang me
   In the house where I sojourned,
55 Greeting You by name each night, Adonai,
   As I have observed Your Torah.
56 Grant me this:
   That I have kept Your precepts.
57 Holdings with Adonai have I;
   I promised to keep Your words,
58 Hoping for Your favor with all my heart:
   Show me grace according to Your word.
59 Heeding my ways,
   I turned my feet toward Your testimonies,
60 Hurrying, never delaying,
   To observe Your mitzvot.
61 Hemmed in by the cords of the wicked,
   I have not forgotten Your Torah.
62 Halfway through the night I arise to give thanks to You
   For the results of Your justice.
63 Happy am I to befriend all who revere You
   And who observe Your precepts.
64 How full is the earth of Your covenantal love—
   Teach me Your statutes!
65 I, Your servant, have been dealt well with by You,
   Adonai, according to Your word.
66 Instruct me in the goodness of judgment and knowledge,
   For I have trusted in Your mitzvot.
67 I used to err, before I was afflicted,
   But now I have been keeping Your word.
68 Indeed, You are good and You do good—

Teach me Your statutes!

69 Insolent men have plastered falsehood over me—
   I will guard Your precepts with all my heart.

70 Immobilized by foolishness is their heart—
   I delight in Your Torah.

71 It was good for me that I was afflicted,
   That I might learn Your statutes.

72 I find the Torah of Your mouth good for me,
   Better than thousands of pieces of gold and silver.

73 Joining me together has been the task of Your hands—
   Give me understanding that I may learn Your mitzvot.

74 Joyfully will those who revere You review me,
   For I have hoped in Your word.

75 Just are Your judgments, Adonai—I know this,
   And You have afflicted me in faithfulness.

76 Join Your covenantal love to me to comfort me,
   According to Your word to Your servant.

77 Join Your compassion to me that I might live,
   For Your Torah is my delight.

78 Jeering people will be shamed, who have corrupted me with lies,
   But I will meditate on Your precepts.

79 Journeys of return may those who revere You make to me,
   And those as well who know Your testimonies.

80 Just let my heart be whole through Your statutes,
   That I might not be put to shame.

81 Keep me, through Your deliverance, from wasting away!
   I have hoped in Your word.

82 Kindle light in my failing eyes through Your word,
   For I say, "When will You comfort me?"

83 Knotted up though I am, like a wineskin in smoke,
   I have not forgotten Your statutes.

84 Know You how many are Your servant's days?
   How long before You will mete out justice to those who
      pursue me?

85 Knaves have dug pits for me—
   Which is not in accord with Your Torah!

86 Keystones of faith are all Your mitzvot;

Enemies pursue me falsely—help me!
87 Killers almost seized me on earth—
But I did not abandon Your precepts.
88 Keep me alive with Your covenantal love,
And I will keep the testimony of Your mouth.
89 Long ages, Adonai,
Has Your word stood fast in heaven.
90 Linking the generations is Your faithfulness;
You established the earth that it might stand forever.
91 Laws have enabled them to stand today,
For all things are Your servants.
92 Letting Your Torah be my delight
Has kept my affliction from destroying me.
93 Long ages have I not forgotten Your precepts,
For You have given me life through them.
94 Loyal to You, I cry: Deliver me!
For I have sought out Your precepts.
95 Louts have waited wickedly for my destruction—
I consider Your testimonies.
96 Limits have I seen to all perfection—
Your mitzvot are boundless.
97 Much have I loved Your Torah!
It is my contemplation all day long.
98 Mitzvot make me more wise than my enemies,
For they are mine forever.
99 More than my teachers have I become wise,
For Your testimonies are my contemplation.
100 More than the elders have I discerned,
For I have guarded Your precepts.
101 Moving my feet from every evil path,
I have sought to guard Your word.
102 Move away from Your judgments? I have not!
For You have guided me.
103 Mellow is Your word to my palate—
More than honey for my mouth!
104 My discernment has grown from Your precepts;
Therefore I despise every false path!

105 Night You turn to noon for my feet;
   Light You provide for my path.
106 Noting my oath, I will uphold it,
   To observe the judgments based on Your justice.
107 Numbed sorely by my affliction,
   I ask You, Adonai: preserve my life according to Your word.
108 Note with favor, Adonai, the freewill offerings of my mouth,
   And teach me Your judgments.
109 Now my life is always in my hand,
   Yet I shall not forget Your Torah.
110 Nefarious people have set a trap for me,
   But I shall not stray from Your precepts.
111 Nurturing the heritage of Your eternal testimonies,
   I find in them the joy of my heart.
112 Noble heart: incline to perform God's statutes
   Forever, at every step.
113 Opposite opinions in the same person I despise,
   But Your Torah I love.
114 Only You are my refuge, my shield;
   I hope for Your word.
115 Out of my way, evildoers—
   Let me guard the mitzvot of my God!
116 Offer me support according to Your word, that I may live,
   And do not shame me out of my hope.
117 Overflow with aid for me, that I may be delivered,
   That I may gaze upon Your statutes forever.
118 Overpowered are all who err in Your statutes,
   For they are deceivers, liars!
119 Offensive dross, all the wicked of the earth,
   You have destroyed;
   Therefore I love Your testimonies!
120 Overcome by terror, my flesh bristles,
   And I am afraid of Your judgments.
121 Practices of justice have I done;
   Do not leave me to my oppressors!
122 Pledge good support for Your servant—
   Let not the arrogant oppress me.

123 Pity my eyes—they fail, seeking Your deliverance
And Your just word.

124 Practice with Your servant according to Your covenantal love,
And teach me Your statutes.

125 Provide understanding to me, Your servant,
That I may testify to Your testimonies.

126 Prepare to work for Adonai:
They have overturned Your Torah.

127 Precisely for this reason do I love Your mitzvot—
More than gold, more than pure gold.

128 Precisely for this reason I affirm every precept on every point—
Every false path I despise.

129 Quaking, I am awed by Your wondrous testimonies!
Therefore I guard them with all my being.

130 Quiet light opens through Your words,
Giving understanding to the open-mouthed.

131 Quivering I opened wide my mouth—
I longed for Your mitzvot.

132 Quickly—turn to me and show me grace,
As is Your practice for those who love Your name.

133 Quicken my footsteps through Your word,
And let no wickedness rule over me.

134 Quash my oppressors, redeem me from them,
That I may observe Your precepts.

135 Quarry light from Your presence for Your servant,
And teach me Your statutes.

136 Quivering streams run down from my eyes
For those who have not observed Your Torah.

137 Righteous are You, Adonai,
And upright are Your judgments.

138 Righteousness You required for Your testimonies,
And great faithfulness.

139 Raging zeal has undone me,
For my oppressors have forgotten Your words.

140 Refined to its purest is Your word—
And Your servant loves it!

141 Raw and despised am I—
I have not forgotten Your precepts.

142 Righteousness on Your part is justice forever,
And Your Torah is truth.

143 Restraint and restriction have struck me,
But Your strictures are my delight.

144 Righteous and just are Your testimonies forever;
Give me understanding that I may live.

145 Sounded I a cry with my whole heart: *Answer me, Adonai,*
Your statutes I will guard!

146 Sounded I a cry to You: *Deliver me,*
That I might keep Your testimonies!

147 Since before dawn broke I arose and cried out;
I waited for Your word.

148 Since before the night watch began, my eyes were open
To contemplate Your word.

149 Strain Your ears to hear my voice, according to Your
covenantal love;
Adonai, sustain my life according to Your judgments.

150 Seekers of sin are drawing near—
They are far from Your Torah.

151 Seekers after You, Adonai, know You are close,
And all Your mitzvot are true.

152 Since old times I have known of Your testimonies,
For You established them forever.

153 Turn Your eyes to my affliction and deliver me,
For Your Torah I have not forgotten.

154 Take my case and redeem me,
Sustain my life for Your word.

155 Transgressors know deliverance is far away,
For they have not sought out Your statutes.

156 Teeming is Your compassion, Adonai;
Sustain my life according to Your judgments.

157 Thousands pursue me, oppress me,
But I have not turned aside from Your testimonies.

158 Traitors have I seen and loathed—
They were not watchful of Your word.

159 Take note that I love Your precepts;
Adonai, sustain my life according to Your covenantal love.

160 Truth is the beginning of Your word;
   Your every righteous judgment is eternal.

161 Underlings have pursued me without cause;
   My heart is in terror of Your word.

162 Uplifted by Your word am I,
   Like one who finds great spoil.

163 Untruths I despise, abhor—
   Your Torah I love.

164 Uncounted times each day I praise You
   For Your righteous judgments.

165 Unimagined peace have they who love Your Torah,
   And there is no stumbling for them.

166 Utterances of hope I voiced for Your deliverance,
   And I have done Your mitzvot.

167 Unabashed, I kept Your testimonies—
   I love them so much!

168 Undaunted, I have kept Your precepts and Your testimonies,
   For all my ways are before You.

169 Visit my cry, Adonai; let it draw near to You;
   Give me understanding, according to Your word.

170 View my petition, let it come before You;
   Deliver me according to Your utterance.

171 Vivid praise my lips would speak
   Because You teach me Your statutes.

172 Voice God's words, O my tongue,
   For all the mitzvot are just.

173 Valiant hand of God, be a help for me,
   For I have chosen Your precepts.

174 Verily I have desired Your deliverance, Adonai,
   And Your Torah is my delight.

175 **Vivify me and I will praise You,**
   And let Your judgments assist me.

176 Vainly have I strayed, like a lost lamb; seek out Your servant!
   For I have not forgotten Your mitzvot.

▶ See also Psalm 4.

מִמִּזְרַח־שֶׁמֶשׁ עַד־מְבוֹאוֹ מְהֻלָּל שֵׁם יְיָ׃

Graduations

PSALM 113

Graduation is a moment to look back at all we have accomplished and all that has brought us to this moment. It is not only a completion; it is also a commencement of the next chapter that we have been preparing for with so much anticipation, effort, and hope.

1 *Hall'lu-Yah!*
Sing *Hallel*, you who serve Adonai—
Sing *Hallel* to the name Adonai!

2 May the name Adonai be blessed
From now until eternity, in this place and every place!

3 **From the sea where the sun rises to the sea where it sets,**
***Hallel* is sung to the name Adonai:**

4 High above all the nations is Adonai,
God's glory is beyond the heavens.

5 Who is like Adonai, our God,
Who ascends on high to dwell,

6 Who descends down low to look
Upon the heaven and the earth?!

7 God raises the submerged from the dust,
Elevates the needy from the ash heap,

8 To dwell with nobles,
The most noble of the people,

9 Inviting the childless woman in the house to dwell
As though she were a joyful mother of children everywhere:
Hall'lu-Yah!

▶ See also Psalms 20 and 128.

יְגִיעַ כַּפֶּיךָ כִּי תֹאכֵל אַשְׁרֶיךָ

Professional Achievements

PSALM 128

In many ways, our work can define us. Often the transitions from learning to leading to expertise pass by unnoticed, until a change, an accomplishment, or a unique success prompts us to realize the milestones we've reached. This psalm invites us to celebrate our achievements—great and small—with pride and gratitude.

1 A Song of Ascendings.
   Happy is everyone who holds God in awe,
   Who walks in God's ways.
2 **When you eat from the toil of your hands,**
   Happy will you be and it will be good for you;
3 Your wife will be like a fruitful vine
   In the innermost parts of your abode;
   Your boys and girls will be like olive shoots
   All around your table.
4 Behold—thus shall the person be blessed
   Who holds God in awe.
5 May Adonai bless you from Zion
   And may you look upon the good of Jerusalem
   All the days of your life,
6 Beholding children for your children—
   Peace upon Israel!

▶ See also Psalm 72.

Retirement

PSALM 112

Retirement can be a time of great joy, and it can also include a measure of fear: fear of losing an essential part of our identity; fear about our legacy; fear that it is now up to us alone to shape a new sense of meaning and purpose. With this psalm, we pray for direction at this moment of transition.

1 *Hall'lu-Yah!*
  Acclaimed are creatures who revere Adonai!
  Beloved in their eyes are God's commandments.
2 Conquerors will their seed be in the earth,
  Devoted, upright, a blessed generation.
3 Enrichment and plenty will fill their homes,
  Forever will their justice stand.
4 Glowing in the darkness, a beacon to the upright,
  Honoring God's lesson of grace, compassion, and justice.
5 Innately good are the souls who lend graciously,
  Judiciously ordering their affairs,
6 Knowing they will never be moved,
  Long, long remembered as righteous people.
7 Malicious tidings do not scare them,
  Never wavering is their heart, trusting in Adonai;
8 On their heart they rely, never fearing to
  Peer down at their oppressors.
9 Quite generously they give to the poor—
  Righteousness stands with them forever,
  Soaring high in glory is their horn.
10 Transgressors will see and rage,
  Unhappily gnashing their teeth, melting away—
  Zeal of the wicked? Destroyed!

▶ See also Psalm 37.

יְהִי־שָׁלוֹם בְּחֵילֵךְ שַׁלְוָה בְּאַרְמְנוֹתָיִךְ:

Moving into a New Home
or Making Changes to a Home
PSALM 122

Moving, renovating, or building a home is a time of many decisions as we envision our future and work to bring it to life. With this psalm, we give thanks for the work that led us to this moment, accept the imperfections that only we notice, and pray that our homes, like our lives, will be places of wholeness and peace for us and those we love.

1 A Song of Ascendings. Of David.
  I rejoice when they say to me:
  "We are going up to the House of Adonai"—
2 Our feet standing
  In your gates, Jerusalem,
3 Jerusalem rebuilt,
  Like a city joined together!
4 For up to it tribes would travel,
  The tribes of Yah—testimony for Israel,
  To sing praise to the name Adonai.
5 For there sat seats for judgment,
  Thrones for the House of David.
6 Pray for the peace of the City of Peace:
  May those who love you find repose.
7 **May there be peace in your palace,**
  Respite on your ramparts.
8 For the sake of my brothers, my sisters, my friends,
  Let me say: Peace within you.
9 For the sake of the House of Adonai our God,
  Let me seek your good.

► See also Psalm 100.

עִבְדוּ אֶת־יְיָ בְּשִׂמְחָה בֹּאוּ לְפָנָיו בִּרְנָנָה:

Marriage

Psalm 100

Marriage and the rituals marking one relationship as distinct from all others are moments of great joy. This psalm evokes that same jubilation, merriment, and blessing. Even in remembering the brokenness that exists in our world, we pray that the overflowing joy of these precious moments carry us into the future.

1 A psalm of thanks.
Sound *t'ruah* to Adonai, all the earth!
2 **Serve Adonai with delight,**
Come into God's presence with joyful song!
3 Know that Adonai is God,
Who made us, to whom we belong;
We are God's people, sheep of God's pasture.
4 Come into holy gates filled with thanks,
Into the divine courts brimming with praise.
Give thanks to Adonai, praise the Name!
5 For Adonai is good, Your covenantal love is eternal,
Your faithfulness will last throughout the generations!

▶ See also Psalm 117.

Pregnancy

PSALM 139

*Some may reach this moment after a long journey, anxious about compli-
cations and wondering if it will ever feel real. Some may reach this moment
feeling joyful, fulfilled, confident, or relieved. Many will have a mixture
of multiple feelings and experiences. In a moment of many emotions, this
psalm invites us to sense the mystery of life and creation.*

1 For the conductor. Of David, a psalm.
  Adonai, You have searched me and You know—
2 You know my sitting down and my rising up,
  You discern my thoughts from afar.
3 You encircle my path and my quarter,
  You are familiar with all my paths.
4 For there is not a word on my tongue
  But that You, Adonai, know it all.
5 You constrained me behind and before,
  And You set Your hand upon me.
6 Knowledge too wonder-filled for me;
  Unattainable—it exceeds my ability.
7 Where shall I go from Your spirit?
  And where shall I flee from Your presence?
8 If I scale the skies—You are there!
  If I bed down in Sheol—behold, You!
9 If I don the wings of dawn,
  If I abide in the abyss of the sea—
10 There is where Your hand will guide me,
  Your right hand will take hold of me!
11 And should I say, "But darkness will disguise me
  And the light around me shall be night"—
12 **Even darkness does not darken us from You,**
  And night shall give light like the day—
  Darkness shall be like light.

13 For You created my innermost parts,
   You sheltered me in my mother's womb.
14 I will give thanks that I am a child of awe and wonder—
   Wonderful are Your works—
   And my being You know very well.
15 My frame was not hidden from You
   When I was made in secret,
   Woven in the deepest parts of the earth.
16 Your eyes saw my developing shape,
   And all these things are written in Your book
   About the days that were forming, though not one of them
      had yet arrived.
17 How precious are Your thoughts to me, O God—
   How manifold the frame of them!
18 While I count them—they exceed the sand;
   I awake; I am still with You!
19 If You, God, would kill the wicked—
   Men of blood, get away from me!
20 Those speaking of You for a wicked purpose,
   Who rise against You, voicing Your name in vain—
21 I loathe those who unload against You!
22 A total hatred I hate them;
   They have become my enemies.
23 Search me, God, and know my heart;
   Test me, and know my troubled thoughts,
24 See whether I have taken any hurtful path,
   And lead me on a path toward eternity.

▶ See also Psalm 37.

יְבָרֵךְ יִרְאֵי יְיָ הַקְּטַנִּים עִם־הַגְּדֹלִים:

After Giving Birth

PSALM 115

Having reached this long-anticipated moment, we hold both relief and a sense that what lies ahead is still uncertain. Our hearts full with hope for the future, we pray for strength, healing, growth, and in time, the comfort of confidence.

1 Not to us, Adonai, not to us,
But to Your name grant honor—
For Your covenantal love, for Your truth.

2 Why do the peoples say,
"Where, oh where, is their God?"—

3 When our God is in the heavens!
Whatever You desire, You have done.

4 Their idols are silver and gold,
Handmade.

5 A mouth have they, but they speak not;
Eyes have they, but they see not;

6 Ears have they, but they hear not,
A nose have they, but they smell not—

7 Hands, but they feel not,
Feet, but they walk not;
They make no sound in their throat.

8 Just like them are all those who make them,
Who trust in them.

9 Israel: *Trust in Adonai!*
God is their support and their shield.

10 House of Aaron: *Trust in Adonai!*
God is their support and their shield.

11 Those who revere Adonai: *Trust in Adonai!*
God is their support and their shield.

12 Adonai has brought us into the Presence,
   Blessing us:
   May God bless the House of Israel,
   May God bless the House of Aaron,
13 **May God bless those who revere Adonai,**
   The small along with the great.
14 May Adonai cause you to increase,
   You and your children with you;
15 Blessed are you of Adonai,
   The Maker of heaven and earth.
16 The heavens are the heavens of Adonai,
   But the earth God has given to humanity.
17 The dead cannot sing *Hall'lu-Yah*,
   Nor can those who go down to the silent places.
18 So we shall bless Yah
   From this moment till eternity—
   Hall'lu-Yah!

▶ See also Psalms 5 and 121.

כִּי־אֶרְאֶה שָׁמֶיךָ מַעֲשֵׂה אֶצְבְּעֹתֶיךָ יָרֵחַ וְכוֹכָבִים אֲשֶׁר כּוֹנָנְתָּה׃

At a Naming Ceremony

PSALM 8

The moment of naming is a culmination of many months and days of anxiety and uncertainty. We remember those who came before, give thanks for those present in this moment, and revel in the miracle of existence and growth.

1 To the conductor: on the *Gitit*.
A psalm of David.

2 Adonai our Majesty,
How majestic is Your name through all the earth,
Whose splendor resounds across the heavens!

3 Out of the mouth of children—nurslings!—You have
established strength
In the face of Your foes,
To declare a Sabbath from enemy and avenger.

4 **For now I see Your heavens, the work of Your fingers,**
Moon and stars which You prepared!

5 What is a human being, that You should be aware,
A child of Adam, that You should even care!

6 Yet You have made them lack but a little of God;
With glory and honor have You crowned them!

7 You have let them rule the works of Your hands;
Everything have You placed under their feet:

8 Sheep and kine, all of them,
The creatures of my own fields,

9 Fowl of heaven, and fish of the sea,
Gliding through the paths of the seas.

10 Adonai our Majesty,
How majestic is Your name through all the earth!

▶ See also Psalm 112.

גַּם־צִפּוֹר מָצְאָה בַיִת

When a Child Reaches a Milestone of Adulthood
PSALM 84

We give thanks for the moments that help us to see what we have accomplished and how we—adults and children alike—have grown and changed. Though so much ahead is unknown, in these moments we feel grounded, as for a short time some small thing is certain. Though this moment too will pass, we—like the sparrow of the psalm—enjoy a sense of confidence and safety. We pray these feelings stay with us as we go forth.

1 For the conductor: on the *gitit*;
Of the sons of Korach, a psalm.
2 How beloved are Your tents, Adonai of hosts!
3 My whole being is yearning, wasting away
For the courts of Adonai;
Singing, my heart and my flesh go Godward, to the living God,
in joy!
4 **Even a sparrow has found a home,**
And a swallow a nest for herself
Where she has placed her chicks:
Your altars, Adonai of hosts, my Sovereign and my God!
5 Happy are those who hang out in Your house—
They keep on singing *Hallel* to You!
6 Happy a person whose strength is in You—
Highways crisscross their heart.
7 Those who cross into the valley of Bacha
Turn it into a spring;
The early rain cloaks it with blessings.
8 They go from strength to strength,
Each one goes before God in Zion.
9 Adonai, God of hosts—
Oh hear my prayer,
Give ear, God of Jacob—selah!
10 Our shield! Behold, O God,
And look upon the face of Your anointed.

11 For a day in Your courts is better than a thousand!
    I choose standing at the threshold of the house of my God
    To dwelling inside the tents of wickedness.
12 For sun and shield are Adonai, who is God,
    Grace and glory does God bestow—
    No good will the Holy One withhold for those who walk uprightly.
13 Adonai of hosts—
    Happy is a person who trusts in You.

▶ See also Psalm 1.

וַאֲנִי בְּרֹב חַסְדְּךָ אָבוֹא בֵיתֶךָ

Looking Back on a Life-Changing Moment

PSALM 5

Whether this occasion originally brought sorrow or joy, we are strengthened by the ability to mark this moment. This psalm speaks of God's loving-kindness shielding us as we walk the path of life with its many unexpected moments, twists, and turns.

1 Conductor's note: with flute!
A psalm of David.

2 To my words give ear, Adonai,
Hear between the lines
Of my mumbled meditation.

3 Hear the notes of my cry, my Majesty, my God.
How I yearn for You!

4 Adonai, it's morning! Hear my voice!
Morning—I'm laying it all out before You,
I'm scanning the skies!

5 A God who desires wickedness? That's not You—
Chaos, wrongdoing, no longer sojourn with You.

6 Boasters may not present themselves before Your gaze—
You despise all doers of evil!

7 You destroy people who tell lies;
Deceivers, their hands full of blood,
Are like idolaters in Your eyes, God.

8 **As for me, embraced by Your covenantal love,**
I am on my way into Your house—
I bow down in awe
In this space filled with Your holiness.

9 Adonai, lead me through Your righteousness
Because of those who lie in wait for me,
Make Your path lie straight before me.

10 There is nothing proper in the mocker's mouth:
Their inward parts are shattered grooves,
Their throats an open grave,
Their tongue is slippery.

11 Declare them guilty, God!
  Let them fall through their own counsel,
  With the masses of their rebellious acts, may You banish them—
  How they defy You!
12 But let all who take refuge in You rejoice—
  Let them shout with joy forever more!
  You will give shelter to them, and they will rejoice in You,
  They love Your name.
13 You grant blessing to the righteous, Adonai,
  With the shield of Your blessing do You crown them.

▶ See also Psalm 112.

הוֹשִׁיעָה אֶת־עַמֶּךָ וּבָרֵךְ אֶת־נַחֲלָתֶךָ

Making It Safely out of a Precarious Situation
PSALM 28

Emerging from a place of doubt and fear, we are more aware of our vulnerability. Our prayers are ones of gratitude touched by apprehension. This psalm speaks to our yearning for continued safety and strength.

1 Of David.
  I'm addressing You, Adonai—
  My Rock, do not be deaf to me!
  Lest, if Your voice be dead to me,
  I will be compared to those who go down into the Pit.

2 Hear the dirge, the plea, I direct to You
  When I raise my hands
  To the deepest place of Your holiness.

3 Do not drag me down with the wicked,
  With those who work evil,
  Who speak peace with their friends,
  And yet in their hearts have malice.

4 Grant them according to their works,
  According to the fiendishness of their acts.
  According to the works of their hands grant them—
  Give back to them what they deserve.

5 Because they do not pay attention to the work of Adonai,
  Nor to the doing of Your hands,
  Tear them down! Do not rebuild them!

6 Blessed is Adonai
  Who has heard the dirge, the plea, I sound out to You.

7 Adonai is my strength and my shield.
  In God my heart trusted—and I was helped!
  My heart exults; with my melody I will glorify You!

8 Adonai is strength unto him,
  The fortress of deliverance for God's favorite anointed.

9 **Bring deliverance to Your people, blessing to Your inheritance—**
  Nurture them and raise them up forever!

  ▶ See also Psalms 16, 46, and 105.

Reuniting After a Long Time of Separation

PSALM 147

We feel deeply the many emotions—anticipation, anxiety, excitement, curiosity, and more—of this reunion after a long separation. Seeing changes in another reflects changes in ourselves. We are grateful for these moments of reunion and the opportunity to be together again to strengthen the bonds between us.

1 *Hall'lu-Yah!*
   Singing of our God is good,
   Heaping praise on praise is pleasing:
2 Adonai is rebuilding Jerusalem,
   Gathering scattered Israel,
3 Healing wounded hearts,
   Binding up our sores,
4 **Numbering every star in the sky,**
   Giving each a name.
5 How great the Superior of our life, how powerful!
   No number can measure discernment:
6 Adonai restores the humble,
   Casting the callous down to earth.
7 Respond to Adonai: "Thank You!"
   Sing to our God: A Melody for the Harp!
8 For God paints the heavens with clouds,
   Preparing the earth for rain,
   Greening grass upon the mountainside,
9 Laying on food for the great beasts
   And for the baby ravens who can only cry out.
10 Not the power of a horse do You desire,
   Nor a man's shining shanks do You favor—
11 Adonai's favorite is the one who can be reverent,
   Those who find their strength by hoping in Your covenantal love.
12 Jerusalem—praise Adonai!
   Zion—regale Your God!

13 For the Holy One has secured the bars of your gates,
   Giving girls and boys the blessing of being
   Wrapped warm within your walls.
14 God has planted your borders with peace,
   Filling you up with harvests of wheat,
   The choicest grains from the stalk.
15 You send forth Your speech to the earth—
   How rapidly spreads the word of Your word!
16 You send us snow soft as fleece,
   Then frost—You scatter its stinging like ashes;
17 Ice—You pelt us with pieces that pierce us—
   Before Your cold, who can still stand?
18 You send forth Your word—it thaws what is frozen;
   You bring back the breeze—our waters flow again!
19 This word You have told to Jacob,
   Your laws, Your judgments
   To the children of Rachel and Leah.
20 To no other nation have You done this—
   Your laws they do not yet know.
   Hall'lu-Yah!

▶ See also Psalms 31 and 130.

אֶפְתְּחָה בְּמָשָׁל פִּי אַבִּיעָה חִידוֹת מִנִּי־קֶדֶם:

After Studying a Jewish Text

PSALM 78

This psalm reminds us that we are a link in the chain of tradition that connects us through the generations. Through continuing to study our sacred texts, we are connected with those who came before us, and it is now upon us to carry on the responsibility of teaching future generations.

1 A *maskil* of Asaph.
Give ear, my people, to my Torah,
Incline your ear to the words of my mouth.

2 **Let me open with a proverb from my mouth,**
Let me speak riddles from of old

3 Which we have heard and known,
Of which our ancestors told us tales.

4 We will not conceal from our children,
Or from telling the next generation,
Tales of the praises of Adonai
And divine strength,
God's wonders, which the Holy One has done:

5 Setting up testimony in Jacob,
Placing Torah in Israel,
Commanding our ancestors to make them known to
their children

6 In order that the next generation—children yet to be born—
may know,
And stand up and tell the tale to their children,

7 That they might place their confidence in God
And not forget the deeds of God,
But observe the Eternal's mitzvot

8 And not be like their ancestors,
A stubborn and rebellious generation,
A generation whose heart was not firm,
Which was not faithful to the God of its breath.

9 The children of Ephraim handling those who raise the bow
   Turned away in the day of battle;
10 They did not keep the covenant of God
   And they refused to walk in the divine Torah.
11 They forgot Your deeds
   And the wonders that You showed them;
12 Before their ancestors the Holy One did wonders,
   In the land of Egypt, the plain of Zoan:
13 Splitting the Sea and leading them across,
   Standing the waters up like a heap,
14 Leading them in a cloud by day,
   And all night by a light of fire.
15 God split rocks in the wilderness
   And gave drink as from the great deeps,
16 Bringing forth streams from a rock,
   Letting water cascade like rivers.
17 Still they continued sinning against the Holy One,
   To rebel against the Most High in the parched land.
18 They tested God in their heart,
   Seeking sustenance for themselves.
19 They spoke against God saying:
   "Can God set a table in the wilderness?"
20 And so the Eternal struck a rock and waters poured out,
      streams were flowing.
   "But can God give bread as well,
   And provide meat for the people?"
21 Therefore Adonai heard and raged,
   And a fire broke out against Jacob;
   Anger roared up in Israel.
22 For they did not believe in God
   And did not trust in divine deliverance.
23 So the Holy One commanded the skies from above,
   Threw open the doors of heaven,
24 And showered sheets of manna upon them to eat—
   The grain of heaven You gave them;
25 Each person ate the bread of angels.
   You sent them game in great numbers,

26 You dispatched an east wind through heaven
 And drove away the south wind by Your might.

27 You rained down nourishment upon them like dust,
 And winging birds like the sand of the seas

28 Which You sent plunging into the midst of the camp,
 Surrounding Your abode.

29 They ate and were very full
 For You brought them the object of their craving.

30 They were not yet estranged from their craving
 (Their food was still in their mouths)

31 When the anger of God rose up against them;
 You slew the most portly among them.

32 Despite all this, they sinned some more
 And would not believe in Your wonders.

33 So You brought their days to a close with a vapor,
 And their years with sudden terror.

34 When You slew them, they sought You out,
 They turned and sought God out like those who seek the dawn.

35 And they recollected that God was their Rock,
 And God on High their Deliverer.

36 They beguiled You with their mouth
 And with their tongue they lied to You.

37 Their heart was not firm
 And they did not believe in Your covenant.

38 But You of the compassionate womb
 Forgive iniquity and do not destroy,
 Many times turning away Your anger,
 And do not stir up all Your wrath.

39 You call to mind that they are flesh,
 "A wind passing by that does not return."

40 How often they rebelled against You in the wilderness,
 Causing You sorrow in the howling places!

41 They turned back, and tested God,
 They brought pain to the Holy One of Israel.

42 They did not remember Your hand,
 The day You delivered them from the oppressor,

43 That You had placed Your signs in Egypt,
   And Your wonders in the plain of Zoan:
44 That You turned their rivers to Blood
   So they could not drink from their streams.
45 You sent a Swarm against them, which devoured them,
   The Frog, which destroyed them;
46 You gave their produce to the destroyer cicada
   And their toil to the Locust;
47 You killed their vines with Hail,
   Their sycamores with frost;
48 You handed over their Cattle to the Hail
   And their herds to the thunderbolts.
49 You sent against them the wrath of Your anger,
   Fury and indignation and trouble—
   A delegation of messengers wreaking chaos.
50 You smoothed out a path for Your anger,
   And did not withhold them from the Darkness of death,
   But handed their beasts over to the Plague.
51 You smote all the Firstborn in Egypt,
   The first products of their vigor in the tents of Ham.
52 You sent Your people going forth like sheep,
   Guiding them like a flock in the wilderness.
53 You led them to safety that they might not fear,
   And the sea covered their enemies.
54 You brought them to Your holy border,
   This mountain which Your right hand had made.
55 You drove out the denizens before them,
   And cast them into the portion of their inheritance,
   Settling the tribes of Israel in their tents.
56 But they tested and rebelled against God Most High,
   And they did not keep Your testimonies.
57 They turned away, acting treacherously, like their ancestors—
   They turned aside, like a crooked bow.
58 They angered You with their high places,
   And with their godlets they stirred up Your zeal.
59 God heard—and was infuriated,
   And categorically cast Israel aside.

60 You shook off the shrine of Shiloh,
   The tent through which You might dwell among humans,
61 And delivered Your strength into captivity,
   Your glory into the hand of the oppressor.
62 You delivered Your people to the sword,
   And were infuriated with Your inheritance.
63 Fire devoured their young men,
   And no wedding songs greeted their maidens.
64 Their priests fell by the sword,
   And no weeping filled the eyes of their widows.
65 The Superior One awoke like someone asleep,
   Like a strongman overcome with wine,
66 And You smote Your adversaries from the rear;
   Subjecting them to eternal reproach.
67 You cast aside the tent of Joseph,
   And did not select the tribe of Ephraim.
68 You did choose the tribe of Judah,
   Mount Zion, which You love.
69 You built Your sanctuary like the heights,
   Like the earth, which You founded for eternity.
70 And You chose David Your servant,
   Taking him away from the sheep pens.
71 From behind the nursing ewes You brought him
   To shepherd Jacob, Your people,
   And Israel, Your inheritance.
72 And he shepherded them in the innocence of his heart,
   Leading them through the discernment of his hands.

▶ See also Psalm 1.

שִׁיר הַמַּעֲלוֹת בְּשׁוּב יְיָ אֶת־שִׁיבַת צִיּוֹן הָיִינוּ כְּחֹלְמִים:

Traveling to Israel

PSALM 126

Psalm 126 is one of the maalot *psalms—familiar today from the insertion at the beginning of* Birkat HaMazon (Blessing after Meals) *on Shabbat and festivals—and sung by our ancient ancestors as they made pilgrimage and ascended the steps to the Temple in Jerusalem. During our travels to Israel today, these words connect us with the ancient hope of our people and all who continue to dream.*

1 **A Song of Ascendings.**
  When Adonai returned the returners of Zion,
  We were like dreamers;
2 Our mouth was filled with laughter then,
  Our tongue with song.
  There was talk among the nations then:
  "God did great things with these people!"
3 God did great things with us!
  We were so happy . . .
4 Return our returners, Adonai—
  In torrents, turning desert streams to flood!
5 Then those who sow with weeping
  Will reap with joy;
6 Those who trudge the row, sobbing as they strain to lift their
      trail of seed,
  Will march in with song, lifting high their golden sheaves!

▶ See also Psalms 24 and 138.

Psalms for Pain

Inevitably, our lives lead us to challenging places. In these times, the words of the psalms turn into reed baskets on our river and sheltering wings around our shoulders, so that we feel held and supported on our journey. When we struggle with physical and emotional pain or when we find ourselves in a threatening or frightening environment, we seek comfort, support, and shelter.

חָנֵּנִי יְיָ כִּי אֻמְלַל־אָנִי רְפָאֵנִי יְיָ כִּי נִבְהֲלוּ עֲצָמָי:

From Health to Illness

PSALM 6

In this time of vulnerability and uncertainty, we pray that our fears will be eased and our strength restored. We cry out for God's healing presence.

1 To the conductor: on strings, on the eighth.
   A psalm of David.
2 Adonai,
   When anger flares in Your nostrils,
   Do not rebuke me;
   When wrath heats up in You, do not chastise me.
3 **Be gracious to me, Adonai, I am so weak,**
   Send me healing, Adonai—
   My bones tremble with terror!
4 My being trembles with terror,
   More each day;
   And You, Adonai—
   How long?
5 Turn back, Adonai!
   Save my life—
   Let me conquer this
   For the sake of Your covenantal love.
6 For in death there is no record of Your presence,
   In the depths of Sheol who will give You thanks?
7 I groan, I scream—exhausted;
   I make my bed a swimming hole each night,
   With this flood of tears I melt my couch away.
8 My eye clouds over with grief,
   It is growing old watching out for those who harass me.
9 Turn away from me, all evildoers!
   For Adonai has heard the voice of my sobs.
10 Adonai has heard my appeal,
   Adonai is taking on my prayer!

11 As for my enemies, let them hide in shame and tremble
     with terror,
  More each day.
  They will turn back tainted—in a second!

▶ See also Psalms 23 and 46.

לִמְנוֹת יָמֵינוּ כֵּן הוֹדַע וְנָבִא לְבַב חָכְמָה׃

Loss of an Ability

PSALM 90

As we grapple with the loss of an ability that was once an integral part of our lives, we seek comfort, understanding, and guidance in finding new purpose, meaning, and strength. May we embrace this uncharted path with acceptance, patience, and courage.

1 A prayer of Moses, man of God.
   Adonai, You have been a refuge for us in each generation.
2 Before the mountains were birthed
   And You had labored with the earth and the world—
   From the first eternity to the last, You are God.
3 You return each of us to the crushed state from which You
      made us,
   From which You say, "Return, children of the earth."
4 For a thousand years in Your eyes
   Are like yesterday, which passes;
   They are like a short watch in the night.
5 You sweep them away—asleep are they;
   In the morning like grass they sprout;
6 In the morning it blossoms and sprouts,
   In the evening it is cut off and dries up.
7 For we are consumed in Your anger,
   We are terrified by Your wrath.
8 You have set our iniquities before You,
   Our secret sins, into the light of Your countenance.
9 For all our days are spent in Your wrath;
   We finish up our years like a sigh.
10 The days of our years have seventy years in them—
   With strength, eighty years—
   Their pride is toil and sorrow,
   It is shorn quickly, and we fly off.
11 Who knows the strength of Your anger,
   Or Your fury, as fierce as the fear of You?

12 **So let us know how to make our days count,**
And sum them up in a heart of wisdom.

13 Return, Adonai—how long?!
Have compassion on Your servants!

14 Satisfy us every morning with Your covenantal love,
That we may sing for joy, delighting in all our days!

15 Delight us in proportion to the days You have afflicted us,
To the years we have looked at pain.

16 Let Your work appear to Your servants,
And Your glory be over Your children.

17 Let the pleasantness of Adonai our God be upon us,
And the work of our hands—establish it upon us;
The work of our hands, establish it upon us.

▶ See also Psalms 27, 40, and 121.

קַוֹּה קִוִּיתִי יְיָ וַיֵּט אֵלַי וַיִּשְׁמַע שַׁוְעָתִי:

Calling Out for Healing

PSALM 40

In moments when we feel uncertain, when we are in pain, when our options for respite are limited, may the words of this psalm assure us that God hears our cries.

1 For the conductor. Of David, a psalm.
2 **Hoping, I have hoped for Adonai,**
   And God leaned down to me,
   And paid attention to my plea.
3 The Holy One brought me up out of the roaring pit, from the
     sloshing mud,
   Raising my foot upon a rock, my happy steps upon a firm
     foundation.
4 God has placed in my mouth a new song, a praise to our God.
   Many will review it and be reverent, and will trust in Adonai.
5 Happy the man who sets God as his trust,
   Who has not turned aside to arrogant deeds
   Or swerved into lying.
6 Many things have You done Yourself, my God;
   Wondrous things, all Your plans for us—
   Nothing I could tell or say is equal to You—
   They are more than I can count.
7 Sacrifice and afternoon meal offering You do not desire—
   You have opened deep passages in my ears which have heard
     the message:
   Burnt offering, sin offering You have not requested.
8 So I said, "See, I've arrived—
   With the scroll of a book inscribed upon me,"
9 To do Your will, my God, I deeply desire,
   And Your Torah is within my inmost parts.
10 I have proclaimed justice in a great assembly—
   Behold, I did not lock up my lips,
   As you, Adonai, know well.

11 I did not hide Your justice in my heart—
I announced Your faithfulness and Your deliverance.
I did not conceal Your covenantal love or Your truth
When I spoke to a great assembly.

12 And for Your part, Adonai, You did not lock up compassion
from me;
Your covenantal love and Your truth preserve me.

13 For troubles without number have swamped me,
My iniquities have overtaken me—I could not see!
They are more than the hairs of my head
And my heart has failed me.

14 Please, Adonai, deliver me—
Adonai, hurry to my help!

15 Let them be ashamed and abashed together,
The ones who seek to sweep away my life;
Let those who desire my hurt be turned backward and put
to shame!

16 Let their disgrace set them back on their heels who say to me,
He-ach! He-ach!

17 Let those who seek You delight and shine with light;
Let those who love Your deliverance say always,
"Adonai is great!"

18 And I—I am indigent and needy,
But Adonai will include me in the Plan.
You are my help and my rescuer—
My God, do not delay!

▶ See also Psalms 6 and 147.

הָבוּ לַייָ כָּבוֹד וָעֹז:

Experiencing a Climate Disaster
PSALM 29

Each line of Psalm 29 depicts a growing storm. These words, familiar to us from Kabbalat Shabbat liturgy, repeatedly mention God's voice. God's voice here might be understood as in the Book of Genesis, causing all of Creation to upend. However, another perspective reminds us of God's presence even in the midst of chaos. The psalm ends with shalom, "peace"—restoring our faith that we can find enduring wholeness even in the midst of devastation.

1 A psalm of David.
Present to Adonai, O godlike beings,
Present to Adonai resplendence and strength;
2 Present to Adonai the resplendence due God's name,
Bow down to Adonai in the beauty of a holy place.
3 The voice of Adonai—
Over the billows!
The resplendent God has bellowed—
Adonai, above the crashing billows!
4 The voice of Adonai—
In strength!
The voice of Adonai—
In splendor!
5 The voice of Adonai—
Shattering cedars!
Adonai is shattering the cedars of the Lebanon—
6 Making them dance like a spindly calf—
Shaking the Lebanon, all her forests—
Turning Sirion, all of Mount Hermon,
Into a wild, young skipping ox!
7 The voice of Adonai—
Carving leaping sheets of flame!
8 The voice of Adonai—
Tossing up the sands of the desert,

The entire Kadesh desert
Whirling in the air!
9 The voice of Adonai—
Startling the deer, whirling them about,
Stripping bare the forests—
While in the Palace all the populace proclaims:
"Resplendence!"
10 Adonai sat as monarch of the Flood;
Adonai shall sit as monarch for all time.
11 Adonai is giving strength to the people;
Adonai is blessing the people with peace.

▶ See also Psalm 24.

וְעַתָּה מַה־קִּוִּיתִי אֲדֹנָי תּוֹחַלְתִּי לְךָ הִיא:

Experiencing Antisemitism, Racism, Discrimination, or Hate

PSALM 39

This psalm's message reminds us that our existence is fragile. As we find the fortitude to continue to fight for equity and justice, we pray that we are able to be compassionate to ourselves and others in the face of oppression. May we sense that God sees the injustice we face and remains with us in our fear and exhaustion, so we may draw strength, pride, and hope from our faith.

1 For the conductor, for *Y'dutun,*
  A psalm of David.

2 I said: "Let me guard my ways from sinning with my tongue,
  Let me guard my mouth with a bridle
  While a wicked person is still before me."

3 I was mute, silent,
  Stilled, even from speaking the good—
  And my pain worsened.

4 My heart grew hot within me
  While I was musing, it burned with fire.
  I spoke with my tongue:

5 "Adonai, let me know my end
  And the measure of my days—what is it?
  I would know how transient I am.

6 Behold, hand-breadths You have made my days,
  And my transience is nothing before You;
  Indeed, all is vapor; all human beings standing—vapor. Selah!

7 Indeed, people walk about as shadows,
  Indeed, what agitates them is a mere vapor;
  They lay up treasure, not knowing who will gather it.

8 **And now—what do I hope for, Adonai?**
  My hope is for You.

9 Deliver me from all my rebellious acts,
  Set me not as the reproach of the foolish.

10 I was muted, I do not open my mouth,
   For You have done this.
11 Stop beating me!
   I am done in by the blow of Your hand!
12 With rebukes You punish men for their crookedness,
   And like a moth You immolate their most desired things;
   Indeed, everyone is just a vapor—selah!
13 Hear my prayer, Adonai, give ear to my cry!
   To my tear do not be silent,
   For I am a stranger with You, a sojourner like all my ancestors.
14 Peer not at me, that I might show my smile
   Before I go away and am no more."

▶ See also Psalms 27 and 74.

זְכֹר עֲדָתְךָ קָנִיתָ קֶּדֶם גָּאַלְתָּ שֵׁבֶט נַחֲלָתֶךָ

Experiencing Political Violence

PSALM 74

When certainty is shattered and the future unknown, we pray for resilience and wisdom to navigate this tumultuous time of devastation and pain, so we may remain steadfast in our pursuit of peace.

1 A *maskil* of Asaph.
  Why, God, have You rejected us eternally,
  Your anger smoking against the flock of Your pasture?
2 **Be present with Your congregation that You formed from
    of old,**
  The tribe of Your inheritance that You redeemed,
  This mountain Zion in which You have dwelt.
3 Pick up Your steps toward the eternal ruins—
  All the evil the enemy has wrought in the holy place.
4 Your oppressors have roared in Your place of accord,
  They have made their signs the only signs;
5 It is considered like people raising up
  Their axes against a thicket of trees,
6 And the time when together they would smash
  Fine engraved work with axes and hatchets.
7 They have fed to the flames Your holy fortress,
  They have trashed to the ground the tent of Your name.
8 They said in their heart,
  "Let us suppress them altogether!"
  They have burned up all the meeting places of God in the land.
9 "We have not seen our signs; there is no more prophet;
  And no one among us knows how long."
10 How long, O God, shall the oppressor reproach?
  The enemy blasphemes Your name eternally!
11 Why do You pull back Your hand, Your right hand?
  Consume them from the midst of Your bosom!
12 God is my Majesty from of old,
  A worker of deliverances in the midst of the earth:

13 You split the Sea with Your strength;
   You smashed the heads of sea-beasts on the water;
14 You crushed the heads of Leviathan,
   You gave him for food to the people of the wilderness.
15 You divided spring and river in two,
   You dried up ever-flowing streams;
16 Day is yours, night as well,
   You established a luminary, the sun;
17 You sculpted all the borders of the land;
   Summer and winter—You shaped them!
18 Keep this before You: the enemy has scorned Adonai,
   And a foolish people has blasphemed Your name.
19 Don't give over Your dove to a creature of the wild,
   Don't forget Your afflicted creatures eternally!
20 Consider the covenant—
   For abodes of violence fill the dark places of the land.
21 Let not the crushed turn back, ashamed,
   Let the poor and the needy praise Your name!
22 Arise, God, side with Your side—
   Remember the scorn You endure all day from the foolish!
23 Do not forget the sound of Your oppressors;
   The din of those who rise up against You rises up continually.

▶ See also Psalm 27.

כִּי־אַתָּה תָּאִיר נֵרִי יְיָ אֱלֹהַי יַגִּיהַ חָשְׁכִּי׃

In Times of Abuse

PSALM 18

When we feel betrayed, disconnected from our true selves, and all of our being aches with pain, this psalm acknowledges the light within each of us, and our significance, importance, and connection to the Source of light.

1 To the conductor: To the servant of Adonai—to David—who spoke to Adonai the words of this song on the day that God saved him from the hand of all his enemies and from the hand of Saul.

2 He said: I have loved You from the womb, Adonai,
My strength!

3 Adonai is my towering crag, my fortress,
My rescuer.
My God is my rock, I take refuge in the Divine.
My shield, horn of my victory,
My stronghold!

4 Praised—I call out—is Adonai;
over my enemies I will be made victorious!

5 The cords of death are choking me,
Destructive floods
Have swamped me,

6 The cords of Sheol have encircled me,
The traps of death
Have advanced upon me.

7 In my narrow space I cried out: Adonai!
To my God I make entreaty:
May God hear my voice from the palace,
May my entreaty enter God's ears!

8 The earth shivered and quivered
The bases of the mountains shake!
They shivered because God is furious!

9 Smoke has gone up in God's nostrils!
From God's mouth a consuming fire,

Inside the Holy Presence flames leapt from the coals!
10 God stretched out the heavens—and descended!
The feet came closer—beneath them, deep darkness.
11 They mounted a winged figure—and took flight,
Soaring on pinions of wind,
12 Disappearing into secret darkness—
An embracing sukkah
In the night.
Dark waters, thick clouds . . .
13 Blinded by brightness, the clouds cleared away—
Hail and coals of fire!
14 Adonai thundered in the skies,
The Most High unleashes God's voice—
Hail and coals
Of fire!
15 He lets loose arrows,
Volley after volley,
Lightning after lightning,
Scattering everyone.
16 Streams of water appeared,
Baring the foundation of the world.
When You uttered a rebuke, Adonai,
When wind blasted forth
From Your nostril—
17 You were sending a message from on high:
You took me,
You drew me out of waves of water,
18 You saved me from my powerful enemy
And from those who hate me, who ganged up on me.
19 They advance on me on the day of my distress,
But Adonai is my mainstay,
20 Directing me to boundless space,
Delivering me—because God delights in me.
21 Adonai rewards me with divine justice;
According to the purity of my hands, God gives me recompense.
22 For I have kept the ways of Adonai,
And I have not acted wickedly against my God.

23 For all God's judgments are before me,
   I will not turn away from them.

24 I have been wholehearted with God,
   I have kept myself away from wrongdoing.

25 Adonai has given me recompense according to my just acts,
   According to the purity of my hands
   Before the eyes of God.

26 With a loving person, You act lovingly;
   With a wholesome person, You show Your wholesomeness;

27 With a pure person, You reveal Your purity;
   But with the crooked, You show Your twisted side.

28 For You bring victory to an afflicted people,
   But You cast down haughty eyes.

29 **For You light my lamp;**
   Adonai, my God, You make my darkness glow!

30 For with You I can race ahead like a legion,
   And with God I can hurdle a wall!

31 As for God, the Divine path is perfect;
   The speech of Adonai is pure,
   A shield for all
   Who take refuge there.

32 For who is God beside Adonai,
   And who is a Rock save for our God?

33 A God who girds me with courage,
   And sets my path toward perfection,

34 Who makes my feet like deer,
   And upon high places raises me up,

35 Who coaches me in combat, hand to hand,
   That my arm may stretch a bow of brass.

36 You have given me the shield of Your victory;
   Your right hand sustains me
   And Your humility expands me.

37 You enlarge my steps beneath me,
   My ankles have not stumbled.

38 I will chase down my enemies, I will overtake them,
   I will not turn back till they are consumed!

39 I will pummel them till they cannot rise,
    They will fall beneath my feet!

40 You have girded me with strength for the siege;
    You bring low beneath me all who rise up against me.

41 You have given me the necks of my enemies—
    I will destroy those who detest me!

42 They screamed for succor—but none came to save—
    From Adonai, but none answered them.

43 So I crushed them like dust on the wind,
    Like mud from the streets I tossed them out.

44 You rescued me from the quarrels of a people,
    You set me as a chief of nations—
    A people I've never sensed now serve me.

45 When their ears hear of me, they hearken to me,
    Foreign children cringe before me—

46 Foreign children wither away;
    They quake in their hiding places.

47 Adonai lives, praised be my Rock—
    Exalted is the God of my victory,

48 The God who wreaks vengeance on my behalf,
    Whose word subdues peoples beneath me.

49 Giving me refuge from my enemies.
    You raise me up above those who rise up against me;
    From the man of violence
    You rescue me.

50 Therefore I will give You thanks, Adonai among the nations,
    And to Your name
    I will sing out!

51 Who magnifies the victory of Your monarch,
    And shows covenantal love to Your anointed—
    To David and his seed throughout all time and space!

▶ See also Psalm 6.

יְיָ יִסְעָדֶנּוּ עַל־עֶרֶשׂ דְּוָי כָּל־מִשְׁכָּבוֹ הָפַכְתָּ בְחָלְיוֹ:

In Times of Pain

PSALM 41

From a place of physical, emotional, mental, or spiritual pain we cry out for relief and comfort. We pray for the understanding and support of our loved ones—and of God—to know that we are not alone.

1 For the conductor: A psalm of David.
2 Happy are those who harbor concern for the poor:
   Adonai will harbor them when the dark days come.
3 May Adonai guard them, keep them in life,
   Give them happiness in the land,
   And not deliver them to the lust of their enemies.
4 **May God support them on the couch of their disease,**
   In the face of their illness You have overturned their every bed.
5 Each one has said: "Adonai, shower me with grace,
   Heal me, bring back my lustiness, though I have sinned
      against You."
6 My enemies speak wickedly of me:
   "When will he wither away and his name die out?"
7 Anyone who comes to visit speaks in vain,
   Their heart building a heap of vicious tales,
   Then goes outside to tell them all.
8 All who hate me whisper about me to one other,
   They're all against me, they concoct wicked stories about me:
9 "Something horrible is sticking to him!
   He's taken to his bed and he'll never get up again!"
10 Even a person who brought me peace—
   Whom I trusted, who shared my food—
   Has now raised up his heels against me!
11 So now, God,
   Shower me with grace—
   Lift me up, that I may pay them back!
   No—
   Lift me up, that I may make our relationship whole.

12 By this I know that You have found favor with me:
   My enemy has not sounded a horn of triumph over me.
13 In my uprightness You have upheld me,
   You have stood me up before Your face forever.
14 Praised be Adonai, God of Israel
   From the forever before to the forever everlasting—
   Amen!
   And Amen!

▶ See also Psalms 23 and 130.

עֵינִי דָאֲבָה מִנִּי־עֹנִי קְרָאתִיךָ יְיָ בְּכָל־יוֹם

In Times of Loneliness

PSALM 88

In the depths of our loneliness when sadness and anger are closest to us, we cry out for guiding lights to help us navigate the deep darkness of solitude.

1 A song, a psalm of the sons of Korach,
For the conductor: on *Machalat L'anot*.
A *maskil* of Heiman the Ezrachite.

2 Adonai, God of my deliverance,
I have cried out by day and in the night before You:

3 Let my prayer precede me in Your presence,
Incline Your ear to my ringing cry!

4 For my being is mired in miseries,
And my life draws near to Sheol.

5 I am reckoned with those who go down to the Pit;
I am like a man abandoned by those who assist,

6 Cut loose among the dead,
Like the slain splayed out in the grave
To whom no one pays heed any longer,
Who are cut off from Your hand.

7 You have bundled me away in the bottommost pit,
In dark places, in the depths.

8 Your wrath weighs me down,
With all Your crashing waves You afflicted me—selah!

9 You distanced my intimates from me,
You made me like pagan idols for them,
I am bound in jail and cannot break free.

10 **My eye grows weak from isolation,**
I have called upon you, Adonai, every day,
I have spread out my hands to You—

11 Will You do wonders for the dead?
Will shades arise, giving thanks to You?—selah!

12 Will stories of Your covenantal love be spun inside the grave,
Of Your faithful oversight in Oblivion?

13 Will Your wonders be known in the darkness,
    And Your justice in the land of forgetfulness?
14 But I, alive, cry to You, Adonai,
    And in the morning my prayer comes to greet You—
15 Why, Adonai, do You spurn my whole being,
    Hiding Your face from me?
16 Sigh do I, perishing since puberty;
    I have borne Your blows, I am benumbed!
17 Your wrath has passed over me,
    Your terrors have terminated me!
18 They surrounded me like water all day long,
    They hemmed me in together.
19 You have distanced lover and companion from me—
    My intimates are darkness.

▶ See also Psalm 63.

In Times of War or Conflict

PSALM 140

In this time of shock, anger, guilt, and fear, we yearn for safety. We hope we are able to find comfort from our own trauma and lend comfort and support to those grieving and most acutely affected. May the words of this psalm affirm our practice of compassion, empathy, understanding, and forgiveness so we may seek paths to peace.

1 To the conductor, a psalm of David.
2 **Save me, Adonai, from evil people,**
   Deliver me from people of violence,
3 Who plotted evil things in the heart—
   Every day they stir up wars.
4 They've whetted their tongue like a serpent,
   A viper's venom vibrates their lips—selah!
5 Protect me, Adonai, from wicked hands,
   Deliver me from people of violence
   Who have plotted to trip up my steps.
6 The arrogant have concealed a trap for me
   And cords; they have spread a net by the wayside,
   They have set snares for me—selah!
7 I said to Adonai: You are my God—
   Give ear, Adonai, to the sound of my pleas!
8 God, Superior, strength of my deliverance,
   You have shielded my head from the shrieks of battle.
9 Adonai, do not grant any desires of the wicked;
   Do not let their projects prosper, elevating them—selah!
10 As for the head of those who surround me,
   Let the labor of their lips drown them!
11 Let hot coals shower upon them, let them be cast into the fire,
   Into the floods, so they will not rise!
12 A person of loose tongue shall not be established in the land,
   A person of violence, a wicked one, shall be hunted down thrust
      upon thrust.

13 I know that Adonai will give the poor their day in court,
   And establish justice for the needy.
14 Indeed, just people shall give thanks to Your name,
   And decent people shall dwell in Your presence.

▶ See also Psalms 9 and 143.

הוֹדִיעֵנִי דֶּרֶךְ־זוּ אֵלֵךְ כִּי־אֵלֶיךָ נָשָׂאתִי נַפְשִׁי:

After an Argument

PSALM 143

During this time of anger and vulnerability, we recognize our power to hurt others, particularly those closest to us, and feel how easily we can be hurt in turn. May we find resilience and humility in the aftermath of this conflict, so we can listen with empathy, communicate truthfully, and move with compassion toward reconciliation and healing.

1 A psalm of David.
   Adonai, hear my prayer;
   Give ear to my request for Your grace.
   In Your faithfulness, answer me with Your justice.
2 Do not enter into judgment with Your servant,
   For no one alive could be judged innocent before You!
3 For my enemy has sought out my very being,
   Pummeling my personhood into the ground,
   Making me dwell in dark places like those who inhabit infinity.
4 And my spirit is faint upon me,
   My heart is desolate within me.
5 I recall days from of old,
   I meditate on all Your work;
   I contemplate the constructions of Your hands.
6 I have spread out my hands to You,
   My being inclines toward You like a weary land—selah!
7 Hurry, answer me, Adonai—my spirit is failing!
   Do not hide Your face from me,
   For I would become like those who go down to the Pit.
8 Let me hear Your covenantal love in the morning,
   For I trust in You;
   Propel me in this path in which I should walk,
   For walking with You has lifted my life.
9 Deliver me from my enemies, Adonai,
   Walking with You I am concealed.

10 Teach me to do Your will,
  For You are my God;
  May Your good spirit lead me in the land of uprightness.

11 For the sake of Your name, Adonai, restore my life,
  Through Your justice, bring me out of trouble;

12 And in Your covenantal love put an end to my enemies;
  Let all my oppressors perish,
  For I am Your servant.

▶ See also Psalms 9 and 27.

Psalms for Relief

When we reach a moment of respite after a long period of chal-
lenge, we give thanks for having the blessing of time to reach this
day. We pray that these moments will sustain us and help us to
live a renewed sense of gratitude and authenticity.

לָכֵן שָׂמַח לִבִּי וַיָּגֶל כְּבוֹדִי אַף־בְּשָׂרִי יִשְׁכָּן לָבֶטַח׃

From Illness to Health

PSALM 16

Though this transition may not happen all at once and may be fleeting, we give thanks for the times when we feel like ourselves. With humility in this moment, this psalm reminds us that although we do not always feel steady, we can find balance.

1 A *michtam* of David.
Protect me, God—
I have taken refuge in You.

2 I thought to myself: I said to Adonai: "You are my Superior—
There is no good for me but in You."

3 Here's to the holy beings who are on the earth,
And the noble souls, in whom is all my delight.

4 Let the sorrows from others' idols multiply—
They have betrothed themselves to the alien!
I shall not offer their libations—they are poured from blood!
Nor will I take up their names on my lips.

5 Adonai is my portion, my libation;
You uphold my destiny.

6 The boundaries of my life have been marked in pleasant ways;
Indeed, this heritage has become more and more beautiful for me.

7 I will bless Adonai, who has advised me;
Indeed, come night and my innards instruct me.

8 I have set Adonai before me always,
At my right hand; I shall not be shaken.

9 **Therefore my heart rejoices, my self-respect exults!**
My body dwells secure.

10 For You will not abandon my being to Sheol,
You will not let the members of Your covenant behold the Pit.

11 You let me know the path of life,
Fulsome joys are with Your presence.
In Your right hand are pleasant things
Forever.

▶ See also Psalms 6 and 92.

מַה־גָּדְלוּ מַעֲשֶׂיךָ יְיָ

Surviving an Accident

PSALM 92

With renewed awareness of our own fragility, perhaps with some feelings of guilt, our sense of the tiny miracles that make life possible is heightened. Now, observing the world continuing on, we notice all of the opportunities for some small detail to change the course of everything. This psalm shares our awe for the Divine in the mundane.

1 A psalm, a song of the Day of Shabbat.

2 It is good to offer thanks to Adonai
And to sing to Your name, Most High,

3 To tell tales of Your covenantal love in the morning
And Your faithfulness in the nights

4 On a ten-string and on a lute,
On meditative strumming of a lyre.

5 For You have given me joy through Your acts;
Of the work of Your hands I shall sing:

6 **"How great are Your works, Adonai,**
How very deep Your thoughts."

7 An ignorant man will not know,
A fool will not understand this:

8 When wicked people sprout up like grass
And all the doers of iniquity peep through the ground—
They will be stamped out for eternity,

9 But You are on high forever, Adonai!

10 For behold, Your foes, Adonai,
For behold, Your foes shall fall away—
All the workers of iniquity shall be scattered.

11 But You empower me like a wild ox,
I am refreshed in scented oils.

12 My eye can spot those who are watching me,
My ear detects the evildoers rising up against me.

13 A just person sprouts up like the palm,
Growing tall like a cedar in the Lebanon,

14 Planted in the House of Adonai,
   They will sprout nobly in the courts of our God.
15 They shall be fruitful even in old age,
   Green and luxuriant shall they be,
16 Branching out in tales of the uprightness of Adonai:
   "My Rock,
   In whom no imperfection can be found."

▶ See also Psalm 16.

מִשָּׁמַיִם הִבִּיט יְיָ רָאָה אֶת־כָּל־בְּנֵי הָאָדָם:

For Sobriety or Changing a Habit

PSALM 33

Throughout our journeys, Psalm 33 reminds us of the transformative possibilities of God's creative power. It expresses gratitude for the gift of life and the joy that comes from living it fully unburdened. May we continue to be strengthened as we walk this path, knowing that God's love and our determination are greater than any struggle or temptation we may face.

1 Rejoice in Adonai, O doers of justice!
  To those who are upright, praise is becoming.
2 Pluck a thankful God-song on your lyre,
  Let your ten-string sing out to Adonai!
3 Sing a song to God
  So it will sound brand new.
  Offer a *nigun*-tune
  As great as *t'ruah* on the Temple trumpets!
4 For the word of Adonai is upright;
  All Your deeds reveal Your faithfulness,
5 How You love righteousness and justice;
  Your covenantal love, Adonai, fills all the earth.
6 Through a word from Adonai the heavens were made,
  And all their host through a windbreath from Your mouth.
7 You build from the billows a watery wall,
  In Your storehouse You stockpile the deeps.
8 Let all the earth stand in awe of Adonai,
  Let all who live on this planet know You can be feared.
9 For as soon as You spoke, life came to be;
  Once You commanded, a whole world arose.
10 Adonai has confounded the plans of the nations;
  You have turned the schemes of the peoples to naught.
11 The plan of Adonai will stand forever;
  The thoughts of Your heart inform generations to come.
12 Happy the nation whose God is Adonai,
  Blessed is the people You chose for this gift.

13 **Adonai looks out from the faraway heavens,**
All humankind are swept into Your gaze.

14 From Your dwelling place, within and without,
You preside over the course each creature will take,
As we set forth from our dwelling place here on the earth.

15 It is You who shapes our hearts into one,
You who discern the quality of all our deeds.

16 No monarch wins victories by the might of her armies,
No brave man is saved by the might of mere strength;

17 They lie who say horses can make them victorious—
No one escapes through armed might alone.

18 Take note: the eye of Adonai watches over the reverent,
Over those who await God's covenantal love

19 To rescue them from death,
To preserve them in hunger.

20 Our beings wait for Adonai;
You are our help and our shield.

21 In You our hearts are joyful,
For in Your holy name we trust.

22 May Your covenantal love, Adonai, be as great upon us
As the time we have been waiting,
Waiting,
For You.

▶ See also Psalms 4 and 94.

לוּלֵי יְיָ עֶזְרָתָה לִי כִּמְעַט שָׁכְנָה דוּמָה נַפְשִׁי׃

After Coming Out/Inviting In
PSALM 94

As we embrace and share the truth of ourselves and invite others to know who we truly are, we look for reassurance that we are each created in the divine image with a unique purpose and heart full of love. We pray to sense God's unending acceptance and understanding of who we are with courage and hope.

1 God of vengeances, Adonai!
  God of vengeances, shine forth!
2 Raise Yourself up, Judge of the earth,
  Render recompense to the arrogant!
3 How long shall the wicked, Adonai,
  How long shall the wicked exult?
4 When they speak, they spew forth disdain;
  All the doers of iniquity act boastfully.
5 They crush Your people, Adonai,
  They afflict Your heritage,
6 They strangle widow and stranger,
  And commit murder on those without parents;
7 They say, Yah will not see,
  The God of Jacob will not pay heed.
8 *You* pay proper heed, you boorish people,
  And you fools—when will you wise up?
9 Will the One who implants the ear not hear?
  Will the One who shapes the eye not look?
10 Will the One who chastises the nations not reprove,
  Especially the One who teaches human beings knowledge?
11 Adonai knows human thoughts—
  That they are vapor.
12 Happy the person whom Yah takes to task,
  And teaches from Your Torah,
13 To give rest from days of suffering
  Until a pit is dug for the wicked.

14 For Adonai will not forsake the people,
   Nor abandon their inheritance.
15 For judgments shall again be made with justice,
   And all the upright in heart shall go after it.
16 Who will rise up for me among the evildoers?
   Who will stand up for me among the doers of iniquity?
17 **Unless Adonai had been a help for me**
   I would have been ready to lie down in silence.
18 If I were to say, "My foot is slipping!"
   Your covenantal love, Adonai, would support me.
19 When disquieting thoughts rage inside me,
   Your comforting brings me joy.
20 Shall the seat of destruction make alliance with You
   As it shapes mischief through law?
21 They mount an attack against the most just person,
   And condemn the person of innocent blood.
22 But Adonai has been a fortress for me,
   And my God the rock of my refuge.
23 You will bring back their iniquity upon them,
   And put an end to them in their wickedness—
   Adonai our God will put an end to them.

▶ See also Psalms 4 and 84.

אֱלֹהֵי צִדְקִי בַּצָּר הִרְחַבְתָּ לִּי

Living into Our Identities

PSALM 4

Psalm 4 offers assurance and strength as we navigate a world that may not always fully understand or accept us when we live in full authenticity. With these words, we are reminded that God's love is unconditional. We pray that our identities and journeys be affirmed by the knowledge that we are wonderfully made in God's image.

1 To the conductor: on strings.
   A psalm of David.
2 When I call out,
   Answer me, God of my vindication!
   When I was confined,
   You opened broad vistas for me—
   Show me Your grace,
   Listen to my prayer.
3 You people—how long will my honor be humiliated?
   You are in love—with emptiness!
   You chase after falsehood—selah!
4 But know that Adonai has set apart the righteous one
      as God's own—
   Adonai listens when I call out.
5 So tremble, and do not sin;
   Speak with your heart upon your own bed,
   And be silent—selah!
6 Offer offerings of justice, which will gain you vindication,
   And trust in Adonai.
7 Many say: "Who will show us what is good?"
   Show us the light of Your presence, Adonai!
8 You have placed a joy in my heart
   Greater than the seasons
   Whose grain and oil pour out in profusion.
9 In peace I lie down, I am one with sleep,
   For You alone, Adonai, let me dwell in safety.

▶ See also Psalm 118.

רָחַשׁ לִבִּי דָּבָר טוֹב

Holding a Child for the First Time

PSALM 45

Holding a child for the first time fills us with gratitude and awe. We hold an embodied miracle, and the start of a new life chapter unfolds before us. This psalm sings of the beauty and sacredness of family bonds. We pray to be fully present in this moment and that we will cherish the complex and amazing journey that lies ahead.

1 For the conductor: Upon Lilies, of the sons
 of Korach.
 A *maskil*, a Song of Love.
2 **My heart is bubbling with a good word.**
 I say: my work concerns a king.
 My tongue is the stylus of a skillful scribe.
3 You are more gorgeous than any son of Adam,
 Grace is poured into your lips—
 And so God has blessed you forever.
4 Buckle your blade on your thigh, brave battler,
 Gird yourself with glory and glitter.
5 May your splendor prosper—
 Ride forth on words of truth, humility, justice,
 And may your right hand teach you wondrous things.
6 Your arrows are sharp—peoples fall beneath you
 Into the heart of the enemies of the king;
7 Your throne is of God, eternal, forever,
 An upright scepter is the scepter of your realm.
8 You love justice, you hate wickedness—
 And so God your God has anointed you
 With oil of joy, more than any of your comrades.
9 Your garments murmur of myrrh and aloes and cassia spice,
 From ivory palaces string-players please you. . . .
17 In place of your fathers shall be your sons,
 You shall set them for princes in all the land.

18 I will make your name present in every generation;
    For this, peoples praise you forever and ever!

▶ See also Psalm 133.

Feeding a Child

PSALM 136

Psalm 136 repeats "For eternal is God's covenantal love" as a mantra as it retells the story of the Torah, from Creation, through redemption, Revelation, and beyond the wilderness.

1 Give thanks to Adonai, who is good,
   For eternal is God's covenantal love;
2 Give thanks to the God of gods,
   For eternal is God's covenantal love;
3 Give thanks to the Majesty of majesties,
   For eternal is God's covenantal love;
4 To the Maker of great wonders all alone,
   For eternal is God's covenantal love.
5 To the Maker of the heavens through understanding,
   For eternal is God's covenantal love;
6 To the Spreader of the earth over the waters,
   For eternal is God's covenantal love.
7 To the Maker of great lights,
   For eternal is God's covenantal love
8 The sun for sovereignty by day,
   For eternal is God's covenantal love
9 The moon and stars for sovereignty by night,
   For eternal is God's covenantal love.
10 To the smiter of Egypt through their firstborn,
   For eternal is God's covenantal love,
11 Who brought Israel out from their midst,
   For eternal is God's covenantal love,
12 With a strong hand and an outstretched arm,
   For eternal is God's covenantal love.
13 To the parter of the Reed Sea into parts,
   For eternal is God's covenantal love,
14 And caused Israel to cross over in its midst,
   For eternal is God's covenantal love.

15 And threw Pharaoh and his army into the Reed Sea,
For eternal is God's covenantal love.

16 To the pastor of the people passing through the wilderness,
For eternal is God's covenantal love.

17 To the smiter of great kings,
For eternal is God's covenantal love,

18 Who slew mighty kings,
For eternal is God's covenantal love,

19 From Sichon, the Amorite king,
For eternal is God's covenantal love,

20 To Og, king of Bashan,
For eternal is God's covenantal love,

21 And who gave their land for an inheritance,
For eternal is God's covenantal love,

22 An inheritance for Israel, God's servant,
For eternal is God's covenantal love.

23 Who took note of us when we were low,
For eternal is God's covenantal love,

24 And tore us away from our oppressors,
For eternal is God's covenantal love;

25 **Giver of sustenance to all,**
For eternal is God's covenantal love.

26 Give thankful praise to the God of heaven,
For eternal is God's covenantal love!

▶ See also Psalm 45.

אֱלֹהִים יְחָנֵּנוּ וִיבָרְכֵנוּ יָאֵר פָּנָיו אִתָּנוּ סֶלָה:

Experiencing Success After Hard Work

PSALM 67

This psalm echoes the Priestly Benediction, the oldest blessing in Jewish tradition that is considered to be a holistic, complete blessing. We recite this psalm with gratitude for this moment and the hope ahead.

1 For the conductor, with string music.
   A psalm-song.
2 **May God show grace to us and bless us,**
   May the Holy One shine the divine countenance among us—
   selah!—
3 To discern Your direction on the earth,
   Your deliverance among all the peoples.
4 *Let the peoples praise You, God,*
   Let the peoples praise You, all of them!
5 Let the nations rejoice and sing,
   For You will judge the peoples justly,
   And as for the nations on earth, may You lead them—selah!
6 *Let the peoples praise You, God,*
   Let the peoples praise You, all of them!
7 Earth has given forth her bounty,
   May God, our God, bless us.
8 May God bless us,
   And may the ends of the earth fear the Eternal forever.

▶ See also Psalm 48.

יִשְׂאוּ הָרִים שָׁלוֹם לָעָם וּגְבָעוֹת בִּצְדָקָה:

Accepting a New Job

PSALM 72

With excitement and anticipation we look forward to new opportunities for growth and fulfillment. We pray to approach our new role with integrity and a commitment to serve others. May we find success, wisdom, and purpose in the journey ahead.

1 Of Solomon:
O God, share Your judgments with the monarch,
And Your justice with the royal heir,

2 That he may judge Your people with justice
And Your poor with fair proceedings.

3 **Let mountains lift up peace to the people,**
And the hills, justice.

4 May God judge the poor of the people,
Deliver the descendants of the needy,
And crush oppressors!

5 They shall fear You
Throughout the life of the sun
And in the face of the moon, to generation upon generation.

6 May he descend like rain on new-mown grass,
Like showers drippling the earth.

7 May the just person sprout up in his days
And a profusion of peace till the moon be no more.

8 May he rule from sea to sea,
From the Great River to the ends of the earth!

9 May desert dwellers bow down before him,
And his enemies lick the dust.

10 The kings of Tarshish and the islands shall bring back gifts;
The kings of Sheba and Seba shall offer liquors.

11 All rulers shall bow down to him,
All the nations will serve him.

12 For he will deliver the needy person crying out
And the poor soul with no person to help.

13 He will spare the lowly and the needy,
   The lives of the needy he will liberate.
14 From injury and from violence he will redeem them,
   For their blood is precious in his eyes.
15 May he live! May there be many gifts from the gold of Sheba;
   May there be prayers continually on his behalf—
   They will bless him all the day.
16 May there be an abundance of grain in the land
   Unto the top of the mountains,
   May its fruit tremble like the Lebanon,
   And may they blossom from the city like the grass of the earth.
17 May his name stand forever,
   May his name wax great before the sun,
   And may all nations bless themselves by him and call him happy.
18 Praised be Adonai who is God, the God of Israel,
   Who alone does wondrous things!
19 May Your glorious name be praised forever,
   And Your glory fill all the earth,
   Amen—and Amen!
20 The prayers of David son of Jesse are finished.

▶ See also Psalm 128.

כִּי־בְחַנְתָּנוּ אֱלֹהִים צְרַפְתָּנוּ כִּצְרָף־כָּסֶף:

Paying Off a Debt

PSALM 66

*Erasure of debt may come after many months or years and much diligence,
discipline, and planning. This psalm of praise expresses how we have been
challenged and yet endured to reach this moment of life, renewed.*

1 For the conductor, a song, a psalm—
Shout t'ruah to God, all the earth!

2 Sing the glory of God's name,
Name the glory of God's praise!

3 Say to God: "How wondrous Your deeds;
Through the greatness of Your strength,
The knees of Your enemies shall shake before You;

4 The knees of all on earth shall bow down before You;
All the earth shall sing to You—
They shall sing of Your name, selah!"

5 Go and see the works of God,
Whose deeds are fearsome for the children of Adam:

6 You turned the sea into dry land,
They passed through the river on foot—
Let us rejoice in You there!

7 God rules through strength forever,
With eyes that keep watch on the nations;
Let not the rebellious raise themselves up against You—selah!

8 Bless our God, O peoples—
Make the sound of praise be heard!

9 You have placed our being in life,
And have not allowed our foot to falter.

10 **For You have tested us, God—**
You have refined us as like the refining of fine silver;

11 You have taken us in a net;
You have pressed down upon our loins;

12 You let men trample on our heads;
We wrestled fire and water hand to hand;

But You brought us out into relief overflowing.
13 I shall come into Your house with burnt offerings,
I shall fulfill to You my vows
14 Which my lips have uttered
And my mouth has spoken when I was in distress.
15 Fattened burnt offerings will I offer up to You
with the fragrant smoke of rams;
I will prepare a bullock with goats—selah!
16 Go hear, and I shall tell the tale
To all who hold God in awe
Of the handiwork the Holy One has handed down to me.
17 To You my mouth cried out;
Praise of God rolled from under my tongue.
18 Had I seen sinfulness in my heart,
My Superior would not have hearkened;
19 But indeed God has hearkened,
You have attended to the sound of my prayer!
20 Praised be God—
You have not scorned my prayer
Nor Your covenantal love.

▶ See also Psalm 67.

יִשְׂמַח הַר־צִיּוֹן תָּגֵלְנָה בְּנוֹת יְהוּדָה

After Planning a Major Event
PSALM 48

After carefully planning details, managing many moving pieces, and keeping the vision for an event at the forefront of our minds, this is a moment of achievement and relief. We have reached this milestone; our work is complete. We pray that we will share the psalm's desire to enjoy the effort and rejoice in the accomplishment of reaching this day.

1 A song, a psalm of the sons of Korach.
2 Great is Adonai, and greatly praised.
  In the city of God, the holy mountain—
3 A beautiful height, source of rejoicing for all the earth,
  Mount Zion, the expanses of the North—
  Town of the mighty monarch.
4 Amid her palaces reigns God,
  Well known as an invincible fortress.
5 For behold the rulers assembled,
  They marched across together,
6 They saw, indeed they were amazed—
  They rushed to and fro in terror!
7 Trembling seized them there,
  Writhing like a woman in labor.
8 With but a wind sent from the east
  You smash the ships of Tarshish.
9 As we have not shut our ears, so we have not shut our eyes,
  In the city of Adonai of hosts, in the city of our God,
  God has established it forever—selah!
10 We have meditated on Your covenantal love
   In the innermost parts of Your Temple.
11 Like Your name, God, so is Your praise, to the ends of the earth;
   Your right hand is filled with justice.
12 **Let Mount Zion rejoice,**
   Let the daughters of Judah be glad
   Because of Your judgments.

13 Walk around Zion, encircle her,
   Count her towers,
14 Set your heart on her battlement,
   Walk among her palaces—
   That you may tell tales of them to the next generation.
15 For this God is our God throughout all time and space;
   God will lead us evermore.

▶ See also Psalms 19 and 113.

יִהְיוּ לְרָצוֹן אִמְרֵי־פִי וְהֶגְיוֹן לִבִּי לְפָנֶיךָ יְיָ צוּרִי וְגֹאֲלִי.

Moments of Respite
PSALM 19

This psalm—which appears in our daily t'filot (prayers)—contains in its last verse the words, "may [my] words...," our traditional hope that all of our prayers, both spoken and unspoken, be acceptable to God. In this moment of respite, even if it is just for a short time, may we be fully present in the blessing of relief and the feeling of being truly understood.

1 To the conductor: A psalm of David.

2 The heavens tell tales of the glory of God;
   "The work of God's hands!" declares the firmament.

3 Day pours out speech to day,
   Night transmits knowledge to night;

4 No speech, no words,
   Their voice unheard;

5 Through all the earth goes forth their chord,
   To the edge of the planet their words.
   You have set a tent for the sun in their midst,

6 Who, like a bridegroom, strides forth from his chuppah,
   Rejoicing like a muscleman to run the course.

7 His going forth is from the edge of heaven,
   His circuit encompasses at its ends—
   Nothing can hide from his heat!

8 The Torah of Adonai is complete, restoring life;
   The testimony of Adonai is faithful, edifying the simple;

9 The precepts of Adonai are straightforward, rejoicing the heart;
   The mitzvah of Adonai is clear, enlightening the eyes;

10 The awe of Adonai is clean, standing forever;
    The judgments of Adonai are true, altogether just—

11 More desirable than gold, than much pure gold,
    Sweeter than honey and a honeycomb.

12 Even Your servant is instructed through them;
    In observing them is great reward.

13 Who discerns mistakes?
Cleanse me from hidden errors.

14 Restrain Your servant from presumptuous acts,
Let them not rule over me.
Then I will be complete
And cleansed from great wrongdoing.

15 **May there be favor**
For the words of my mouth and the meditation of my heart
Before You,
Adonai, my Rock
And my Redeemer.

▶ See also Psalms 23 and 67.

לַיָי הָאָרֶץ וּמְלוֹאָהּ תֵּבֵל וְיֹשְׁבֵי בָהּ׃

Before Going on Vacation
PSALM 24

Much preparation leads to vacation. We anticipate having the opportunity to relax and renew during our upcoming time of rest, connection, and adventure.

1 Of David: A song.
To God belongs the earth and its fullness,
The world, and those who dwell within it.

2 For You founded it upon the seas,
You established it upon great rivers.

3 Who shall ascend to the mountain of Adonai
And who shall stand at Your sacred site?

4 Clean hands shall, and an honest heart;
One who raises up no falsehood to deface My name;
Who has not sworn an oath that hides deceit—

5 This one shall raise up a blessing from Adonai
And justice from the God of our deliverance.

6 This is the seed of seekers after You,
These are the ones who look for Your presence,
This is Jacob—selah!

7 Raise up your heads, O regal gates—
Let yourselves be raised up, O doors to eternity!
Let there enter the Ruler of Glory!

8 Who is this Ruler of Glory?
Adonai, strong and mighty;
Adonai, mighty in battle!

9 So raise up your heads, O regal gates—
Raise up the doors to eternity!
Let there enter the Ruler of Glory!

10 Who is this, this Ruler of Glory?
Adonai of hosts!
This is the Ruler of Glory—selah!

▶ See also Psalms 126 and 138.

Index of Psalms

PSALM ..... PAGE

Psalm 1 3

Psalm 3 31

Psalm 4 134

Psalm 5 87

Psalm 6 101

Psalm 8 84

Psalm 9 6

Psalm 13 32

Psalm 16 127

Psalm 18 113

Psalm 19 146

Psalm 20 17

Psalm 23 50

Psalm 24 148

Psalm 27 41

Psalm 28 89

Psalm 29 107

Psalm 31 57

Psalm 33 130

Psalm 34 60

Psalm 37 24

Psalm 39 109

Psalm 40 105

Psalm 41 117

Psalm 45 135

Psalm 46 8

Psalm 48 144

Psalm 50 12

Psalm 55....... 15

Psalm 59 10

Psalm 61 51

Psalm 62 52

Psalm 63 49

Psalm 66 142

Psalm 67 139

Psalm 72 140

Psalm 73 18

Psalm 88 119

Psalm 90 103

Psalm 91 33

Psalm 92 128

Psalm 94 132

Psalm 100 79

Psalm 103 55

Psalm 104 35

Psalm 105 44

Psalm 111 14

Psalm 112 77

Psalm 113 75

Psalm 115 82

Psalm 117 43

Psalm 118 4

Psalm 119 65

Psalm 121 38

Psalm 122 78

Psalm 126 97

Psalm 128 76

Psalm 130 54

Psalm 131 39

Psalm 133 23

Psalm 136 137

Psalm 137 40

Psalm 138 22

Psalm 139 80

Psalm 140 121

Psalm 143 123

Psalm 144 27

Psalm 147 90

About the Author

Rabbi Jade Sank Ross grew up in Kinnelon, New Jersey, where she spent the majority of her days divided between the local stables riding horses and her Jewish home, Barnert Temple, in Franklin Lakes, New Jersey. It was because of her involvement at Barnert Temple and because of the mentorship of Rabbi Elyse Frishman, Cantor Regina Lambert-Hayut, and Director of Lifelong Learning Sara Losch that Rabbi Sank Ross discovered her calling as a rabbi.

Rabbi Sank Ross received her BA in anthropology and international and global studies from Brandeis University, where she was also a member of the a cappella group Company B. She was ordained as a rabbi in 2018 by the Hebrew Union College–Jewish Institute of Religion in New York, where she earned awards for her achievements in homiletics and human relations.

Having previously served under her mentor Rabbi Howard Goldsmith as the assistant rabbi and director of education at Congregation Emanu-El of Westchester in Rye, New York, Rabbi Sank Ross currently serves The Community Synagogue in Port Washington, New York.

Rabbi Sank Ross is passionate about cooking and baking. This passion, combined with her love of Jewish learning and community, has led her to contribute to three Jewish Food Hero cookbooks by Kenden Alfond.

Rabbi Sank Ross is married to Rabbi Daniel Ross, and together they are most proud to be Adina and Bella's parents.

www.ingramcontent.com/pod-product-compliance
Lightning Source LLC
Chambersburg PA
CBHW070331090426
42733CB00012B/2441